100
DEVOTIONS

Happiness

TO BRIGHTEN
YOUR DAY

PUBLISHING GROUP

NASHVILLE, TENNESSEE

978-1-5359-4593-6

Published by B&H Publishing Group ·
Nashville, Tennessee

2 3 4 5 6 7 8 · 23 22 21 20 19

Contents

Introduction

Before you even start reading, turn on the television. If you take the time to flip through a few of the channels, you'll probably notice that there are few if any stories about happiness. We are a people that focus on the negative in the world. The news tells us the world is going to end on a daily basis. Television shows discuss heartbreaking conflicts that the characters seem to be found trapped. Even some of our children's stories are engulfed in a sense of despair. We live in a world that seems to be focused on the concept of negativity. For some people, the glass is not half-empty. The glass is broken, incapable of ever coming back to a place where it can be fixed. For many of us, living in a world with this kind of focus can lead us to holding on to a mind-set of defeat. After all, how can one find victory in a world that has such a focus on defeat? How can we ever have hope in a world where hope seems pointless?

The point is that God did not call us to lose our joy. He does not want us to be a people that have been defeated by the ways of the world. He does not want us to be a people that refuse to see the happiness that He has given to us. Forget about what's on the television and look at your life. Count your blessings and realize all of the good that God has given you. Do not allow yourself to be overcome with sadness. Instead, take on a spirit of joy over the things that God has obviously given you as a blessing.

You probably have a loving family, or at least friends that love you like family. You have people that care for you and people that you so easily care for. You have people that aspire to give you love, and you have love that you are so willing to give to people. You have been forgiven for wrongs and because of that you have been able to forgive others. You have had moments of peace, harmony, and protection during moments of hardship. Whatever it may be, many of us have been blessed to the point where we can look out and be thankful over all of the things that God has done in our lives.

That is why this book is here. It is filled with little reminders that we are blessed; that we are given so much to the point where being happy and joyful are merely the by-products of all that God has given us. Even though the world may say we have nothing that should make us happy, with a little bit of thought, we quickly realize that God has proven that sentiment wrong. Read this book daily, and allow yourself to be reminded of the good in your life. Take the good that God has given you and respond with thankfulness, joy, and, above all, happiness.

1

Love Unmatched

*For God loved the world in this way: He gave his
one and only Son, so that everyone who believes
in him will not perish but have eternal life.*

JOHN 3:16

Finding love, in one form or another, has always been a priority. In today's time, however, it seems like the entire world is telling us to find love, or at least show it in some way. Our culture has different sites on the internet that point us to our matches based on questionnaires and algorithms designed to pair us with that special someone. People seek counseling in order to resolve past conflicts with their parents and how to better love them. Parents are encouraged to read book after book on how to love their child the "right" way, whatever that means. Even some of our favorite movies and television shows paint us a picture of the kind of love that we should find. We live in a world that seeks love . . . that desires to love and be loved, but there is a love that is so much more than what this world gives or could ever give.

That love comes from God. We are constantly chasing after love, and sometimes, we never realize that there has always been a love, unmatched, that has always been chasing after us. There is a love that has been on our heels since the day we were born, just waiting for us to turn around. There is a love that performed the impossible. There is a love that gave that which could not be given. There is a love that has loved you in spite of you and your blemishes;

a love that only asks you to believe. This love is eternal. This love always has been and always will be. This love is God's love.

It goes, without saying, that God has a love for us that we will never understand. God loved us so much that He gave His only Son for us. He gave His Son to die on a cross so that we may have eternal life through His Son. There is a love there that none of us will ever understand. We think about Christ and how He loved us enough to die for our sins, but we rarely ever think about God's love. We rarely ever think about the fact that God loved us so much that He gave His only Son for us so that we might live. When I think about the love of a parent, the level of God's love becomes unfathomable. It is something that we will never understand. An older pastor was once heard saying this statement, "Like Christ, there are people on this planet that I love enough to die for them, but there is not one of you on this entire planet that I love enough to give my child's life in exchange for yours."

When we have taken into account the level of love that God has for us, we cannot help but have a more positive outlook on our lives. Happiness and joy are some of the things that are simple by-products of the love that God has for us.

Let us thank God for this love; this love that cost
everything, and yet, we pay nothing.

2

Broken Spirit Dries You Up

A joyful heart is good medicine,
but a broken spirit dries up the bones.
PROVERBS 17:22

⌐⁓⌐

L ife has often been described as an adventure or a roller coaster. There are many highs and lows, many ups and downs, but it seems that we often get so focused on the lows and the downs that we cannot even begin to recognize the ups and the highs. We do not ever really take the time to recognize the good in our lives. Sometimes we get brought down in life. That is a fact of life that most of us have come to know, if not all of us. We can't turn off our brains. We can often fixate on the negative moments that the world can bring. Sometimes our hearts are left broken. Relationships end. Loss happens. Obstacles seem insurmountable. There are many things in the world that break us from time to time. There are things that bring us down, that can't be avoided. What do we do in order to deal with this? We find joy. We find the good. We focus on the silver lining of the dark clouds that seem to loom over us.

People all over the country have said time and time again that there is always a silver lining. Parents do their best to remind their children that there is always a bright side, and you know, they're right. Sometimes when we have a dark cloud looming over us, we so often forget that the sun is right behind it. Even when looking in the mirror we may find a face that others find beautiful, but all we can see is the blemish that just won't seem to go away. Some of us may have a stellar performance at work or in school, and yet, within all of the success, there is a focus on the failure in one's performance. More often than not, we are surrounded by the things in which we can find positivity, but we choose to obsess on the negativity.

Simply put, we have to look at the positivity. We have to be willing to look past the negativity and do our best to find the joy in life. Even when it's hard, we have to find the good in the bad. We have to be willing to find the peace hidden in the desperation. Though the hard times may come, we have to remember the moments that bring us the most joy. It may sound cliche, but we have to be willing to look at our glasses as half full instead of half empty. This is often the best thing you can do in order to live a life of happiness and joy.

So what are we going to do? Find the joy and let that bring us to our feet, or will we settle in our brokenness and let our spirit wither?

Pray for God to give us the wisdom to find the joy
in the bad times, so that we may not stay in those bad times.

3

Your Strength from Him

Do not fear, for I am with you, do not be afraid,
for I am your God. I will strengthen you; I will help you;
I will hold on to you with my righteous right hand.

ISAIAH 41:10

~~~

There are days that require the right strength to get through. Whether we're dealing with a hard time at work, our kids are needing us more than what we have to give, there are bills we have to pay, people we have to care for; it's exhausting. With all of this going on sometimes it's scary for us to just get out of bed in the morning. Where do we find the strength? How are we able to stand up, look at the morning sun, and take the steps toward accomplishing all of the tasks that are waiting for us?

It's hard to believe sometimes, but our strength is not our own. The strength that we have is a kind that has been given to us. There is a strength that we could never attain on our own. This strength is one that comes from God that gives us the ability to climb the mountains we face every day. This strength is one that keeps our heads above the work we would be drowning in otherwise. The Bible tells us that we have nothing to be afraid of because our God is a God that strengthens, helps, and holds onto us with His hand. Even when the day is hard, we can rest and have joy in knowing that God is with us.

That is the point of the strength; that God is with us. No matter how many assignments we have thrown on our desk, or how many meetings we have to attend, or how many people we have to take care of, God is with us, and when God is with us, so is His strength. We should remember that the next time we feel like we cannot handle something on our own, that we are far from alone. We are never alone when we reside in Him and He in us. It is a concept that most of us have probably been made aware of, or have developed a sense of familiarity.

Remember that when life seems to be giving you nothing but curveballs, God will not allow you to strike out, and if He does, this failure is not permanent. We were not made to be weak. We were made to be strong, but the only way we can have the kind of strength to take on the obstacles that wait for us each and every day is to place our strength in Him, to place that strength in God. It is only through God that we will ever be strong enough to take on the trials of the day.

> Lord, thank You for not leaving me on my own
> and being with me always. Thank You for giving me
> strength, and please continue to do so. Amen

4

Jesus Overcame

"I have told you these things so that in me you
may have peace. You will have suffering in this world.
Be courageous! I have conquered the world!"

JOHN 16:33

~~~

It feels like we are living in some of the roughest of times. If we were to turn on the television right now and watch the news, we would probably notice that not one of them ever really looks happy anymore. People are constantly worried about who's going to war with whom. They worry about the future of our country as well as others. They speculate on which dictator is getting ready to invade another country. The constantly bring up reports on what crime was committed by whom. We see people suffering every day. It feels like everyone is suffering in this world. No one seems to be happy with the way the world is anymore, or at least, we don't ever really get a chance to see that happiness on television the way we once did. It can often seem that the negativity of the world is blotting out the light of the positive.

How can we move forward when the world seems so dark? How can we ever expect to find the light when there is so much darkness? It may seem a little too easy, but all we have to do is simple. We have to be willing to adjust our perspective. We have to be willing to realize that the world we are living in is a defeated one. It has been beaten. The issues of this world have already been overcome. How is this, you may ask? It is through Christ's sacrifice that the world has been beaten. Christ conquered the world when He died on the cross and gave His life for us. The worst thing that the world could ever throw at us was death and destruction, and still, Christ conquered that through His death and resurrection. It was at that moment that the world was defeated. Sin had been defeated! It is because of His sacrifice that today we can take heart in knowing this.

When we look around this world, what do we see? Do we see a broken world that we are inevitably doomed to reside in, or do we see a world that our Savior has already beaten? Do we see a world that.has long been defeated? It is a bit easier for us to find joy in the world when we know our team has already won. Even though there are times that may frustrate us, we must remember that we are only part of a world that holds no power over us. Christ died so that we would not be taken down by this world. In that knowledge, we can't help but to have a more positive outlook.

Lord Jesus, thank You for dying for my sins. Thank You for saving me from this world. Continue to give me courage as I walk through a world that You have conquered. Amen

5

We Have Everything We Need

And my God will supply all your needs according to his riches in glory in Christ Jesus.
PHILIPPIANS 4:19

~

We live in a world of want. We live in a world where people are always striving for more than what they have. Sometimes, for some of us, it feels as if there's just not enough. We feel that there is something missing. There are never enough hours in the day; no matter how hard we work, we sometimes have to live with the fact that we only have so much time to finish our work. There's never enough money left over. No matter what we do, we always seem to always need just a little bit more. Sometimes it may feel like we're just trying to swim to the top of a pool that people just keep filling up with more water. It feels like we just can't catch a breath, but we can find joy in knowing that God has given us everything that we could ever need through His Son. We may not have the fancy car, the Pinterest perfect house, or the job that seems to be perfect for us, but think about what these things are for a moment. They are wants. As much as we hate to admit it, wants fade. That car will be too old, that house will need repairs, and that job will only satisfy you for so long. God is not a supplier of wants. He is a supplier of needs.

We never really take the time to think about it, but there is a great deal of truth in that verse. How many times has it felt like we're not going to be able to make ends meet and yet, we do? Money may be a little tight, but God always finds a way to bless our needs in such a way that we are able to make it to the next paycheck. Some of us feel like our jobs are in jeopardy at all times. You may show up a couple of minutes late every now and again, but you still made it regardless, and some of us are blessed enough to have great coworkers or a boss that we respect, or even work that we love. There might have been a car repair you had to pay for, but somehow, you found the money, and even though that car may not be the nicest model or exactly what you wanted, it has four wheels and you're able to get to wherever your destination may be. You may have said you didn't have the time to finish a project, and yet, you still found a way to finish it. Sometimes we have so little faith that we can have our needs met, but we can be joyous in knowing that all of those needs are met, in one way or another.

May we pray in thankfulness to God for meeting all of our needs. May we be reminded of what are wants and what are needs. May we remember that in the toughest of times, our needs will be met.

6

Overflow with Hope

*Now may the God of hope fill you with all
joy and peace as you believe so that you may
overflow with hope by the power of the Holy Spirit.*
ROMANS 15:13

Hope is one of the most amazing emotions we could ever feel. Think of a child going to their favorite place to eat. The day for that child seems to be a day that is filled with magic. Think on a Friday at work, everyone is in a better mood because of the fact that the hope of the weekend is approaching quickly. There is a special joy that comes from hope. We find joy in opening gifts because there is a hope in what is under the wrapping. The same kind of joy is found in giving gifts because we hope our loved ones cherish what we have given them. Joy is found in having a meal with loved ones; there is a hope that comes with the approach of good food and good conversation. We find joy in many different ways, but hope holds a special kind of joy.

We have mentioned the joy that comes from gift giving, good meals, and family. Why is this? It's because there is an excitement, an ecstatic, electric happiness that comes from hope.

With hope, we find that there is a joy over the future; there is a faith. We take joy in preparing meals, finding gifts, and planning journeys for the people that we love because we have faith that there will be joy shared when we finally get to serve those very people we love. Hope, simply put, is the faith in the joy to come.

Now, we may all hope in many things. Some of us put our hope in people, in our jobs, even in pleasant times to come, but there is a difference between hope and faith. Faith is a form of assurance. Many of us have probably been let down from time to time by the things that we've placed our hope in; we have had people let us down, plans have fallen through, and sometimes the weekend is not all that we had hoped it would be. There have been so many times that we've all felt that faith is not real. People will feel like they should not have a sense of hope at all. This is a problem because, in all actuality, we have probably just not put our faith in the right things.

When we put our faith in God, we find that something incredible happens. We find that we have put our faith in the one thing that will never let us down. Life may let us down from time to time, but how good is it that we are able to have a God in whom we can always place our faith, and never be let down.

Lord, thank You for hope. May I be reminded constantly
that there is a joy in hope, a joy in faith, a joy in You.

7

In Person

*Though I have many things to write to you, I don't want
to use paper and ink. Instead, I hope to come to you and
talk face to face so that our joy may be complete.*

2 JOHN 1:12

Reunions are some of the happiest times in most people's lives. Whether it be for family, school, or just a group of friends coming together, there is an excitement about getting together with old friends. There is a joy over being with people face to face. This is difficult for us today because we live in a world that is engulfed in electronic communication. The whole truth of it all is that sometimes a message, text, or phone call just isn't enough. Sometimes there is a joy that is overflowing in our hearts that only drives us to share what is going on in our lives with others, or we have found out something incredible that has happened in the lives of the ones we care about and it only seems right that we want to share in that happiness with them. Whenever you experience a deep happiness, it just doesn't seem right to simply go home and send a text message that says you have had a good day. An email does not even come close to the level of connection you would want to have with loved ones. There is a desire to celebrate. There is a longing to share the joy we have with others. Whenever we come to a place of delight, it is almost instinctual for us to want to enjoy that moment with those that we love dearly.

When we get a promotion, a certification, a raise, the kids got good grades, or the boss liked something we have done at work, or even something as simple as us making it to the weekend, we don't normally think about going home and sitting on the couch and texting or calling our friends and family about the blessings we've received. It is not that these messages are necessarily bad in their essence. It is simply that a message or a phone call never seems to be enough. There is a desire for us to be face to face with the ones we love.

Celebration was never something that was meant to be carried out on one's own. A celebration is meant to be shared with the ones you love in person. When the weekend has come, or a special occasion is on the horizon, or even the most wonderful moments have come up and surprised you, don't settle for a nod to the good and move on to something else. Joy is something that was meant to be shared with others; it was never meant to be something that is to be kept to oneself. So go out and share that joy with others.

Father, encourage me to recognize the good in life.
Encourage me, further, to share the joy that comes
from that goodness with those around me.

8

Fixing the Problem

"I tell you, in the same way, there will be more joy in heaven over one sinner who repents than over ninety-nine righteous people who don't need repentance."
LUKE 15:7

The attitude that we are supposed to have in today's world is one that says, "Everything's okay!" It's hard to admit that there is ever such a thing as a problem, especially when we feel like the whole world is watching our every move. We tell ourselves that we have to keep it together for our families, kids, friends, coworkers, boss, and many others, but what do we do when there's something wrong in our lives? How do we handle the problems that we're struggling with? We are left with a decision. Do we try and act like we're fine? Or do we admit that we have a problem?

It's a strange occurrence. The entire world will generally tell you that it is so important for us to admit when we have a problem. Every single person will agree that is normally the first stance that we should take. What normally seems to happen, however, is that whenever a person is confronted with an issue that they may possess, they are very quick to show us how everything is completely fine, and when I say they, I mean us. It is never an easy task to be willing to take the first step to repentance. Even though all of us know that we are only human, we seem to have so much trouble in admitting that we're not perfect, or worse, we will admit to flaws that we have that are not really at the root of what the problem actually is. It's like a cleptomaniac admitting that they have a problem with jaywalking occasionally. There is a reason why it is often difficult to arrive at a stage of repentance. We must first, however, discuss what repentance actually is. Repentance is the act of feeling sincere remorse over a wrongdoing and an attempt at making sure that it doesn't happen again. Christ is clear that there is a great joy that follows this act, and we all know that. Ask any former addict, they will tell you how they would never want to go back to the life that they used to lead. There is a strength and a joy in repentance.

When we admit that there is a wrong in our life, it is never a happy moment at that time, but joy does come. It comes when we've moved past the problem and moved forward with Christ. It is a lot like climbing a mountain of one's own pride. The climb is never present, but ask any mountain climber, and they will tell you that the view is always worth it.

Father, I know I don't do what is right from time to time. Help me to repent, Lord, so that I may find joy and peace with You.

9

The Right Word at the Right Time

A person takes joy in giving an answer;
and a timely word—how good that is!
PROVERBS 15:23

⌒

There was once an older gentleman that lived in a neighborhood of young families. We have probably seen this before. Older homes are sold and young families come in and update the homes. It brings new life to the neighborhood, but the older generations have been known to feel out of place whenever these new changes occur. The older gentleman, however, had spent years watching his old neighbors be replaced by new ones. He feared that he would have nothing in common with these new neighbors, so he simply worked out of the shop in his garage—fixing pieces of furniture as well as making new pieces. He always enjoyed working with his hands and had developed a side business selling his furniture at neighborhood yard sales. It was his only interaction with his new neighbors at first, but to his surprise, he found a lot of the young people at his door over the next few months seeking advice on carpentry. It was something that brought the man tremendous joy and allowed good friendships regardless of the age between him and his new neighbors.

The right words can make all the difference in the world some days. Whenever you are working in difficult times, a word of wisdom, encouragement, or comfort can bring much-needed peace and joy. Sometimes the right words can even bring an end to what feels like a lifetime of frustration and anxiety, but more often than we would like, these words lose their strength. People become too busy to really listen, or we can become too fearful to even share those words in the first place. Like the old man, we can often feel like our words are not even worth listening to, and will just keep our wisdom to ourselves.

When you notice those around you that are having a stressful time, do not be afraid to reach out and give them the right words. When you are going through a difficult time, don't push away those that try and comfort you, and don't be afraid to seek out the wisdom of those that have lived a life that you haven't. Sometimes all we need in the most trying of times are the right words, and if we pay attention, there is something more important to this than what we ever realize. The right words can bring light to the most dark situations; they can spark friendships; they can even bring the old into a sense of invigoration. The right words can do a lot, but we've got to be willing to open our mouths and actually use them, or open our ears and actually listen for them.

Lord, thank You for those around me that want to make sure I'm okay. Thank You for their kind words and allow me to hear them. Father, give me the right words and allow others to hear me when I try to comfort them.

10

Out of Darkness, into Light

*But you are a chosen race, a royal priesthood,
a holy nation, a people for his possession, so that
you may proclaim the praises of the one who called
you out of darkness into his marvelous light.*

1 PETER 2:9

Have you ever been lost? Have you ever felt like you couldn't find the light at the end of the tunnel? Most of us can probably remember a time when we've literally been in darkness. I can remember a time as a child when there was a storm and the power went out. I remember being in a state of shock. I felt alone and scared. I was in a different part of the house when I heard my mother calling for me. My hands would trace the walls as I walked slowly to her voice. The closer I got to her, however, the less I paid attention to her voice and the more I noticed the faint light of a flashlight on the other side of the house. At first, I walked cautiously but quickly to that light, but when it was clear that there was nothing separating me from that light and my mother. I ran to her. There is rarely a joy that can match the reassurance that comes from light overcoming the darkness.

There are so many of us that seem to walk in darkness today. This is not the literal darkness that most of us have come to know during the night time, but this is the darkness of walking a path that we don't know. So many of us have had dark times in our lives. We've had to deal with loss, or rejection, or even the darkness of confusion. It is in these times that we seek out a light in our lives. We want to be able to make it out of these dark times. Sometimes it's something as simple as reaching out to loved ones for guidance and wisdom. Sometimes, it's something as difficult as letting something go that you know you need to. Whatever the case is, whenever we've moved from that darkness, we often look back with gratitude—knowing that we were called out of that darkness it and into the light.

Like the flashlight in a power-outage, God shined a light on our path in order for us to find our way to Him. God's light is something that never can be overtaken by the darkness, no matter how dark the moments may seem. When we think about the darkness that we used to walk in, it seems only natural that we should share the knowledge of that joy that we felt when the Father called us out of the darkness into His light.

Father, thank You for calling out in those dark times so that I could find my way back home to You. Thank You for finding me in the darkest of moments and calling me into Your light.

11

Hardship Has Purpose

Consider it a great joy, my brothers and sisters,
whenever you experience various trials, because you
know that the testing of your faith produces endurance.
JAMES 1:2–3

Sometimes we put ourselves in harm's way. That's a given. We start to exercise because we know it's the right thing to do, but everyone who's ever been on a treadmill remembers the first time they ran on one . . . or, in some cases, fell off of one. Those of us that know people that became runners through the process know that there were a grueling few months where every time they would step on the machine, there was almost the guarantee of shallow breaths, tight chests, and aching limbs. Some of us can remember signing up for a class that we knew was going to be difficult but we needed the credit from the class. Some of us can remember the long nights in a library studying for hours on end and feeling like there was never going to be an end to the confusion, frustration, and heartache that came from that class. Some of us remember the hardships that we didn't sign up for, the hardships that were thrown on us without our permission. Some of us have experienced loss, regret, heartache, pain, injury, sickness, and hopelessness. For some reason, however, we can almost always come out of these situations with joy. Why is this? It is because on the other side of hardship is appreciation. Even though there have been times that we've been completely miserable, we look back on those times with an appreciation for what we have because of them.

When we leave the gym after years of work and trust in the process, we move from having a feeling of exhaustion to a feeling of satisfaction. When we have put in weeks of study in a class we knew nothing about, we can walk away knowing that we passed a class we needed in order to form the knowledge that we needed. From loss, we find appreciation for time that we had with that person and for loved ones we have with us now. From regret, we find a new insight and wisdom on how to avoid future mistakes. For all of these instances and others, we gain a stronger spirit for what is to come. These hardships, as much as we don't want to admit it, sharpen us. It's one of the most difficult things to experience personal hardship. It almost always feels like whatever struggle that comes into our lives is, somehow, catered specifically for us . . . but there is a point. Through these hardships comes strength and perseverance, and that is something in which we can always find joy.

Allow us to pray for wisdom, Lord. Give us the knowledge
to know that there is a point to this hardship. That through this
and with You, we will come out stronger. Allow me to look at the
obstacles in my life as an opportunity to better myself through You.

12

Being Kind Means Forgiveness

And be kind and compassionate to one another, forgiving
one another, just as God also forgave you in Christ.
Ephesians 4:32

This seems like a pretty easy thing to say. Being kind and forgiving to each other is something that we've been told since before we were old enough to really speak, but how can something so easy to understand be so hard to do? Why is it so difficult for us to forgive others? A great deal of it is because we feel like they've done wrong to us. Have you ever had anyone do something to you that you can't forgive? You can barely look at them. It makes you angry to think about the fact that they never said, "Sorry." With this level of anger and frustration that we have with others, we find ourselves in an area where we are constantly moving around forgiveness. We see it as this grand mountain that we have to climb, and it just seems easier to move around it. This, however, is not the case, and even though it may be a difficult thing to do, not forgiving others can have terrible consequences.

What does this do? What are these consequences of unforgiveness? For one, It enslaves you to this person that you've decided doesn't deserve your forgiveness. This person owns your joy and happiness. Because you have not forgiven this person, you've allowed this person to have control over you.

Whenever you see them, your heart beats faster, you face becomes flushed, and you can't even seem to look them in the eye. Because you have chosen not to forgive someone, you have given them a power over your life that few ever have. If someone hurts you, and you hold onto that memory of hurt and can't move past it, then you will never have happiness or joy around that person, and it will only stay that way unless you can forgive them. That is the tragedy of unforgiveness. It is not that you have given this person control over the negative emotions in your life; it is that you have robbed yourself of any future happiness with this person. Because of our unforgiveness of others, we can never really appreciate what it means to have future joy around this person or even with this person.

Something we also need to remember is this. We're not perfect either. We are so far from it. What all do you think Christ had to forgive for your sake? We have to be willing to remember that not one person on this planet is perfect, but there is no joy where there is no kindness, and there is no kindness where there can be no forgiveness.

Father, instill in me a desire to forgive those who have wronged me. Instill in me a desire to seek out forgiveness from those that I have wronged so that I may find joy in them and above all, in You.

13

We Will Desire in What We Find Delightful

Take delight in the LORD,
and He will give you your heart's desires.
PSALM 37:4

⁓

There are so many things that we desire in this world. Some of us open our closets and realize that we haven't been shopping in about a year. Some of us get in a car that is older than we are. Some of us look around at all of the things in life that we could ever want. Whenever we get on social media we see people that seem to have everything that they could ever ask for: the perfect job, the perfect spouse, the nice house, the cool car, and all of the other things that come from the materialistic side of things. We may say that we would never want all of these things, but we would all be lying if we said that we didn't want any of it. There is something to be said about this. Our heart will naturally desire the things in which we find delight. If we delight in the world, our heart will naturally desire the things of the world, but If we delight in God, our desires may look very different.

There are a few things that we should point out here. It is true that if we take delight in God, He will give us what our heart desires, but there is something about this verse most people get wrong. Some of us look at this and read it backward. Some of us will think to ourselves, "I'll get what I desire if I just delight in the Lord." This is true, but think about who God is. If we think that God will bless us with a beach vacation or a cabin getaway in the mountains, then we are not looking at God the way He is. If we think that we will get the newest model of a car or the biggest house in town, we are not exactly looking at who God is. We might be in danger of turning Him into a genie.

When we find our delight in the Lord, we start to naturally seek out the things that the Lord wants as well. It's the same as anything else in life. When you delight in your spouse, you desire the things that benefit your marriage. When delight in your job, you desire the things that benefit your career, but when we delight in the Lord, our desires start to reflect Him. Things like helping and loving others become just as delightful to us as that beach trip so many of us are almost desperate for.

Take time to work on what you find delight in; you may just be surprised at what it will do to the desires of your heart.

Lord, thank You for all that You do. Allow me to find my delight in You so that my desires are reflective of You and not of the world.

14

We Take Joy in Salvation

*"Indeed, God is my salvation; I will trust him and
not be afraid, for the LORD, the LORD himself, is my strength
and my song. He has become my salvation. You will
joyfully draw water from the springs of salvation."*

ISAIAH 12:2–3

So many times we are told about how we should find Joy in God's love. It is something most of us have heard, but very rarely do we take the time to process the kind of love that God has given us. We don't ever really think about what salvation means. It is one of those *churchy* words that few people ever take the time to look up what it means. It is one of those words that we have heard so many different times. It is a word that we understand the meaning of, but if you were to ask most of us for its definition, they would probably return the request with a blank stare. Simply put, it means to save or protect someone from something. It means to remove us from harm, destruction, risk, or loss. God loves us so much that He gave us salvation. He gave us protection. He saved us and removed us from something awful.

This brings up an important question. What are we being protected from? How have we been saved? It's definitely not a happy topic to discuss. It's probably the least happy topic ever. To put it bluntly, God saved us from hell. He saved us from an eternity of pain and emptiness. In short, He saved us from the one place where He is not. He saved us from the worst place imaginable.

Why did we need to be saved from it? Because of our sin, we were destined for hell. How did He save us from this? Well, He sent His Son to die for us so that we would not have to spend our eternity there. When we think about that fact; when we take a moment to realize that God saved us from the worst thing possible, it is something that we should naturally respond to with joy. I, typically, think about it on the same level as being saved from a fall. I've seen parents do it all of the time. A child will lose their balance and put themselves in harm's way, and yet, the parent will, almost out of instinct, remove the child out of harm's way, even if it means putting themselves in danger to do it.

Think about salvation. Think about what it actually means, and notice that salvation is what God wanted for all of us all along. God did not want us to suffer; He wanted us to be redeemed. When we take the time to do this, a joyful spirit is simply a by-product.

> Allow me to take note of all that You have done
> for me, Lord. Allow me to truly know and understand
> what salvation means, and respond in joy.

15

By Faith into Grace

*We have also obtained access through him
by faith into this grace in which we stand,
and we rejoice in the hope of the glory of God.*

ROMANS 5:2

~

I once a knew a girl in my neighborhood growing up that had the only trampoline in the neighborhood. It was something that made her one of the popular kids in the neighborhood. We would all be there almost every day after school and jump on the trampoline. One of the boys, however, tried to be funny and jumped out of a tree onto the trampoline. (A thing only boys would do, I might add.) When he landed, the trampoline, mainly because of years of playing on it, broke. The boy was uninjured, but he ran away from the house as soon as it was broken. After days of hiding out, his mother found out and forced him to go and apologize immediately and offer to work to pay for a new one. When the boy came to the parents to explain what happened and apologize, the parents only asked, "Well, are you alright?" The boy was shocked, but then the mother said, "I've watched you play on that trampoline for years with my daughter and you've always been so kind to her. I care about you more than that old trampoline." The boy did not have faith in the girl's parents and expected condemnation.

There are so many different occasions in life that we mess up, that we make mistakes. We do the wrong thing. Even when we don't mean to, there is still a time where we fall. We let others down. We hurt people that we care about. We say the wrong thing. Sometimes it's an accident, but other times, if we're honest, we can be harsh to others. We know we are not supposed to be this way. We know how we are supposed to treat others, and yet, if we're honest, we probably hurt someone just about every day. When we think about it, it is something that can often make us feel as if we don't deserve grace or love.

Our mishaps can often make us wonder how God can love us when we have these mishaps from time to time (or more often than that). We often feel that, because of our sins, we are unlovable. We have to remember, however, that that is not how God is. He does not love us because of our actions. He loves us in spite of them. Even though we have these poor moments, God still loves us. Through our faith in Him and His Son, God gives us grace. Even in the moments where we are far from perfect, God still gives us grace, and it is that grace that we find hope and happiness.

Lord, thank You for loving me when I am unlovable.
Thank You for giving me grace in the moments when I don't deserve them. Allow me to give grace to those around me.

16

Good Can Come with the Bad

*So I take pleasure in weaknesses, insults,
catastrophes, persecutions, and in difficulties, for the sake
of Christ. For when I am weak, then I am strong.*
2 CORINTHIANS 12:10

One of the most frustrating things about being a Christian in this world is the ridicule that we often have to go through. Some of us have seen the level of social persecution that Christians deal with on a daily basis. Students are made fun of in school for having their Bibles out. Coworkers can respond to witnessing with a sense of sarcasm, and the world, in general, does not respond to favorably to the actions of Christians. Some of us have experienced frustrating conversations with people that try to poke holes in the logic of our faith. Many of us have learned that something as simple as praying over a meal can be met with mockery, but that's the way the world is in a lot of ways. People that don't believe don't always know how to feel about what they don't understand. When they see people that are different from them or their way of life, they don't naturally want to know what makes them different so much as it may just simply offend them. When they come across Christians, they don't always come with questions. Sometimes, they only bring negativity, and in that negativity, we need to respond with a perspective of positivity.

So why is this a good thing? Why is this something in which we should find joy? For one reason, it is how we were told to respond. We are not called to be people that fall into depression whenever the world doesn't like what they see. We are a people that have been called to be triumphant, even in the most depressing of times. As strange as it may seem, weakness is a standard judged by the world. What I mean by this is that something that may be seen as a weakness in the eyes of the world is often seen as a strength in the eyes of God. It may be seen as a weakness to pray over a meal or to say that you'll pray for someone. It may be seen as a weakness to read the Bible when the rest of the world classifies it as a two-thousand-year-old book, but it is in those "weaknesses" that God finds strength. It is within our weaknesses according to the world that God sees strength. We are called to look past what the world sees and do our best to look into what God sees. So when you see a fellow Christian out in the world, do you see weakness in them putting themselves out there, or do you see a strength in standing out in the world for God?

Father, thank You for my strengths and allow me to see
what others call weak as something that is strong. Allow me
to look at what the world calls weakness as strength.

17

The Pure Heart Sees God

"Blessed are the pure in heart, for they will see God."
MATTHEW 5:8

~

A father stood in front of his little girl and wife for advice. It was something that he had become accustomed to doing. The question for that particular day was to wear the blue tie or the black tie. The wife said black because it was formal for the meeting he was going to be attending and that it might help him match his boss's attire, but the little girl said blue. When he asked why, she simply said that it was "shiny and made Daddy look pretty." The father decided to go with the daughter's advice. When his wife asked why, the father simply said: "She chose the tie because she only saw me, she didn't care about the other stuff." The wife smirked and kissed him and said, "Well, it does make you look pretty." It's incredibly difficult to rule out a pure heart because you know any intentions that come from those with a pure heart come out of love.

Whenever we think about what it means to be pure, a lot of us put many different notions in our minds. Some of us may think that purity comes from the people with whom we come in contact. Some of us think that it is about being self-righteous. Being pure, however, is about being free of sin or malice. We, however, are not talking about our lives necessarily, we are more so talking about our heart. So we must ask ourselves, what does it mean to be pure of heart, and how do I show a pure heart?

It is a simple solution. To be pure in heart means to actively chase after God. It means to honestly love others. It means to hope for the best in other people's lives. This may be simple, but it is, by no means, an easy task. Loving people is often not easy. We have all been very difficult to love, but Christ loved us in spite of ourselves.

Many are unwilling to live a life that follows after Christ's example, but those of us that are willing to take up that challenge are able to receive something that is priceless. We do not mean that we will literally see God and speak with Him the same way that others did, it means more so that we will see His work and have an appreciation and happiness over what we are able to see. To be pure of heart means to love unequivocally and to hope the best for those that you love. It means to have intentions that cannot be questioned. With a pure heart, we notice goodness on a level that few ever will. The ordinary hearts see goodness as an accident; the pure see it as divine.

Lord, give me a pure heart and instill in me a spirit that chases after You in all that I do. Allow me to love others without selfish intentions, and allow that love to show me the goodness that You give every day.

18

Love with Your Actions

*Little children, we must not love in word
or speech, but in action and in truth.*
1 JOHN 3:18

~~~~~

We've all heard it before: "Talk is cheap." This is something that many of us believe to our cores. Married couples have dealt with this sentiment time and time again. Spouses often hear the other spouse say that they want to be shown how much they are loved, not just told. Friendships are put in jeopardy when they say they are best friends and yet don't take any time to work on their friendship. The actual portrayal of love is something that has become reduced in our time. It seems that people throw the word "love" around to every ear that will choose to listen. The word has become cheapened. This is not to say that love isn't powerful. It is the most powerful thing in the world, but our mouths throw it around as quantity, and our actions show it as quality. So the question is simple. How do we show love through our actions? Do we let our mouths take care of it, or do we actually get up and show it?

Saying that we love someone is the easiest thing that we could ever do, but showing someone that we love them is not that much harder. This is something that few agree with at first. A great deal of us believes that the only way to truly show love is through grand gestures. You don't have to rent out an entire restaurant, buy an expensive trip, or even get a tattoo to proclaim your love for someone. All it takes is a little bit of going out of your own way. Write a note to someone you love. Give a hug unexpectedly. Be there for someone when they need you. We all know when we are loved by the way people act around us. When people look us in the eye when we're talking, when people smile at us when we come into the room, or when people simply acknowledge our presence, that can go a long way in showing one's love for us. This is not necessarily romantic. You can do any of these forms of love for someone you care about, but don't just settle for words. Think about how special you feel when someone initiates a reunion, or invites you to be a part of something, or even chooses to sit with you in a time of need. God wants us to do so much more than simply send a text to check in, or to "like" something they've posted. Showing love is not like climbing a mountain, it is more like simply walking at an incline. Anyone can do it. To put it bluntly, if you say you love someone, act as if you mean it.

Allow me moments that will put me in places and
opportunities to show love for others and allow
me to recognize when others show love to me.

19

Happiness Comes to the Wise

*"How happy are your men. How happy are
these servants of yours, who always stand
in your presence hearing your wisdom."*

2 Chronicles 9:7

Most of us know of that older person in our church who just seems to have a wealth of wisdom and knowledge. Most of the time they are seen wearing a faint smile as if they are just aware of all of the mysteries of life. You can always see the mark of this wisdom because there is normally a joy shown by the person that has received advice on a topic that they were confused on. These are very special people in your church. What makes these people special, however, is not their knowledge so much as it is their willingness to share that knowledge.

It is one of the most amazing feelings in the world when you finally get just the right piece of advice that you were looking for. Whenever trouble is on the rise, we often have a person, a confidant, whom we can go to with trust in hopes of finding wisdom for the questions that confuse our brain. These people in our lives are the ones who bring us a great deal of joy because of the fact that they are often people that care enough to tell us the truth and share with us their thoughts on how to handle a certain situation.

The same can be said on our end. Whenever people seek out our wisdom, there is a joy shared between ourselves and the people asking because of the fact that they have come to know that we are people that love and care for them enough to tell them what the right thing to do is. There is a joy in being trusted. There is a happiness that grows between you and the people that seek your wisdom, or you and the people whose wisdom you seek. Why does this joy exist? It is because of the fact that wisdom is a precious commodity. It is something that few people have. Some of us know plenty of smart people that don't have any wisdom. It is something that can only be gained through experience. So for people to share that wisdom, they are sharing something that is precious. They are sharing something that they are only willing to share with those that they love. To put it mildly, wisdom is shared in the same regard as love. You can only be seen as precious for people to share what is precious to them.

Don't be afraid to seek out the wise. People that share their wisdom are, more often than not, some of the most caring individuals we could ever hope to find.

Lord, thank You for the wise people in my life. Thank You for allowing me to have wise friends and family to seek out in my time of need. Help me to share my wisdom when people seek it, and allow me to be grateful when wisdom is given to me.

20

Discipline Is Given Out of Love

See how happy is the person whom God corrects;
so do not reject the discipline of the Almighty.

JOB 5:17

⌒

D iscipline is one of those aspects that no one likes. The reason is because of the fact that we have twisted its meaning to the point at which we start to see discipline as punishment. It doesn't matter what the discipline is over, because we view it as a form of punishment, we tend to only look at discipline as something that is negative. Most of us have felt this way ever since we were children.

Growing up, many of us probably hated being disciplined. It is one of the most unpleasant things for children to go through, but with it, comes a purpose, or it should at least. What does it actually mean to be disciplined? It is not the same as punishment, even though most of us probably look at it as such. Punishment is simply negative. There is not a positive found in punishment and there isn't supposed to be a positive. Punishment is meant to be negative and that's all, but what exactly is the positive in discipline? What makes it something that is good? The outcome is what is important. In the outcome of discipline, we find correctness, and in that correctness, we find happiness.

Discipline comes with the purpose of making something better. A coach disciplines a player by making him or her run laps. A teacher disciplines a student when he or she asks a student to stay after class. These may be unpleasant things, but they are not punishments. After weeks and weeks of running those laps, the athlete will find that they are much faster. After hours and hours of tutoring, the student will find out that their grades are starting to improve. During the time of this discipline, the student and the athlete probably assumed that they were being punished, but that could not be farther from the truth. If you were to ask them now, they would probably tell you that they appreciated their time of discipline because of the fact that it is what had made them better. A person will never get better at anything unless he or she is willing to undergo the discipline it takes to get better.

Discipline may very well be something that is unpleasant, but there is a point to it. The more we take on discipline, the more we will find that we are getting better at what we aspire to be. As said before, discipline is not normally looked at as something that is pleasant, but it is the outcome of that unpleasantness that we find a correctness, a betterment, that brings happiness and joy.

> Lord, allow me to look to the discipline in my life and see
> it as an opportunity to get better. Allow me to recognize
> that discipline is not a form of punishment. Allow me to
> respond to discipline with happiness and graciousness.

21

The Happy Understand

The one who understands a matter finds success,
and the one who trusts in the LORD will be happy.
PROVERBS 16:20

~

When a new assignment is put on one's desk, a supervisor will normally expect the worker to respond with a certain attitude. The worker will either tell their boss that they will either find a solution to the problem presented or they will say that they cannot handle the obstacle placed in front of them. The attitude does not necessarily have to do with one's knowledge. After all, many of us have probably had challenges thrown at us that we didn't know how to accomplish, and yet, somehow we figured out how to find a solution to what needed to be done. The successful people in the world normally have a spirit of understanding that they will either already know how to solve an issue or they will gain the knowledge necessary. There are those of us that either have, or are willing to gain, the understanding necessary to confront the issues ahead of us, and those of us that do not. If we're honest, these people are easy to point out not so much because of their ignorance, but more so because of their level of frustration when confronted with problems.

As mentioned previously, whenever a problem is set before us, we normally will find two types of people: the one that understands and the one that scratches their head. We probably have seen or been these types of students in math class. A teacher writes a problem on the board and asks for a volunteer to solve it. The one that has not taken the time to familiarize themselves with the material will stare at the board and struggle through the problem in frustration, but the one that has studied and trusts in their knowledge will write down the answer confidently and take a happy pride in their work. Their level of knowledge was not what determined their level of confidence as much as it was centered around their willingness to gain that knowledge and understanding.

The same kind of thing can be said about our relationship with God. Problems will arise in all of our lives; that is one of the most common parts of life. How we respond to these problems, however, makes all the difference in the world. Those of us that trust in God will typically have a more positive outlook on life. Our trust in Him will make us happy and get us through the tough moments. That trust, however, is built through a constant seeking of a relationship with God. The deeper our relationship is with God, the more we find ourselves having an understanding attitude and a trust in Him. Trust in God and find understanding; you may be surprised at the level of harmony that comes from a trusting relationship with Him.

Lord, instill in me a spirit that trusts in You. Allow me to look
at the problems in life with a spirit that relies on You.

22

God Has a Plan for Us

"For I know the plans I have for you"—this is the
LORD's declaration—"plans for your well-being,
not for disaster, to give you a future and a hope."
JEREMIAH 29:11

There are so many days that we wake up and turn on the television and find that the news isn't what we want it to be. We see stories of war. Countries that barely have enough to sustain themselves are going to battle with each other. We see stories of desperation. Refugees are seeking asylum from the flawed government running their home country. We see stories of famine, people starving because of a lack of abundance. People die in storms. Politics rule the screens. It seems that every day is one that is filled with chaos, and sadly, sometimes we let that chaos seep into our lives, and we feel as if we cannot escape all that is happening in our lives. When we live in a world that is filled with negativity, we can sometimes assume that it is only a matter of time before the doom that rules this world will fall upon us if it hasn't already. That is not the plan, however. It never has been the plan. As Christians, we know that God has a plan for us, and that plan is one that is filled with hope.

Although it may seem difficult, this is something that we should hold onto as a reminder in life. We should take the time to acknowledge that no matter how chaotic the world may seem around us, God has a plan for us. That plan is not one that will lead to disaster; it is one that is promised to lead to a future of welfare and of hope. This does not mean that goodness will necessarily fall from the sky if we believe hard enough. It does mean, though, that the disaster of the world is not according to His plan. God does not want us to suffer; He loves us. Why would anyone ever want loved ones to suffer? What we have to be willing to come to terms with is the fact that we are called to have faith in Him. It is in this faith that we realize that the future God has for us is one that is filled with hope. The world may seem like it is engulfed in doom. It may feel as if the world is only a few bad decisions away from ending altogether, but this is not the way for us to believe. God has not given us an ending, but rather, a future. Have faith in the God that is bigger and stronger than the chaos of the world, and find peace and hope in Him and all that He does.

> Father, remind me daily that no matter what happens
> in the world, You have a plan for me. Remind me that this
> plan is one of hope and one that points to the future.

23

We Have a Purpose

He counts the number of the stars;
he gives names to all of them.
PSALM 147:4

⌒

Most of us have taken the time to look at something innumerable and been stunned by it. It is not something that is difficult to do. We stand on the beach and think about the millions of grains of sand that help support us. We see snowfall and are filled with wonder over the number of snowflakes that had to fall in order to get an inch. We look in our front yards and ponder the number of blades of grass that cover the brown earth with green, or as children, we look to the stars and gaze at the uncountable specks of light that fill the black void.

We have all heard stories of people that look up at the sky and realize how small they are. Children, from time to time, will look up at the stars and begin to count. It is only a matter of time before the child notices that the longer they spend counting, the more they realize it is impossible to count all of them. They find that they count the same star twice or the night sky is too vast for them to be able to count all of them. This is not a surprise, of course. Even scientists admit they have not numbered every single star in the universe. All they are able to do is give an estimation, which even they will tell you is probably an underestimation. According to them, there are hundreds of billions upon billions of stars that are able to be observed in the known universe. It is a number, that even though scientists are counting each day, that will probably never be reached in our lifetime or our great-great-great-grandchildren's lifetime.

When we realize, though, that not only has God counted every single star, He has also named them, it allows us to know that God had a plan for all of those stars. God knows every star by name. He knows every single one of us personally. Being known by God changes our outlook when we think about it. There is nothing within God's creation that is without a purpose. For God to know us means that there is a purpose He has for us. We are a part of God's creation, and we are definitely much easier to count than the stars. In knowing we have a purpose, we can find joy. Go out and find out what this purpose is, for God took the time to do more than just count you. God took the time to have a purpose for you. You are more unique than the billions of stars that are visible from our planet, and like God naming them, He has named your purpose as well.

Remind me of my purpose, Lord. Constantly remind me that, like the stars, You know me by name and have a purpose for me.

24

Don't Worry about Tomorrow

"Therefore don't worry about tomorrow,
because tomorrow will worry about itself.
Each day has enough trouble of its own."

MATTHEW 6:34

We have all been there. It is a beautiful Sunday afternoon and yet you cannot seem to even think about enjoying it because all you can seem to think about is the meeting you have on Monday, or you cannot even focus on the upcoming weekend because you are too busy worrying about all of the little things that have to get done before you can even have a time for rest. For some of us, we have even evolved from nervousness to numbness because of the level of anxiety that we have allowed a dwelling in our lives.

People often look to the future with anxiety. It is a common characteristic of our culture. We look out to the world and realize that there are so many different things that they have to take care of. We have jobs to go to, kids to take to school, lunches to pack, families and relationships to manage, and so on and so forth. We also have to deal with the little surprises that we know are just going to pop up at a moment's notice. Anxiety is something that has become a daily part of all of our lives. Some of us can't even seem to start our day without already thinking about the next one, and it's exhausting. Think about the people in your life that are constantly planning for tomorrow. Even the ones that have found a rhythm in this planning live a life of constant running. This life of constant apprehension is not one that God wants for us.

I know what you're thinking. How can I not worry about tomorrow when I have so many different things and people to take care of? The word to focus on in that question is "worry." It's perfectly fine for you to wonder about tomorrow. It's a good thing to plan for the future. There is nothing wrong with that. In fact, we are encouraged to have a hopeful and wise plan for our futures. We think about how to raise children, what we can do to care for others, or how we can show our love to the ones in our lives. Hopeful planning is a wonderful thing. What is detrimental to us, however, is the state of worry. All worry has ever been is just another form of fear. Whenever we worry, we allow the control of our future to be taken away from hope and immediately given to fear, and we were not called to be fearful. So before you start worrying about what your boss has to say or what project your child needs help with, realize that these moments are not even here yet. Let God worry about them. You have today to satisfy.

> Lord, remind me not to worry. Allow me to put my trust
> and future in Your hands so that I can take care of today.

25

You Can

I am able to do all things through him who strengthens me.
PHILIPPIANS 4:13

⌒

Most of us are familiar with this verse. We've seen it in churches, in Christian homes, even painted on some gym walls. It is a verse meant to encourage. That is something in which most of us can find agreement. Where the verse fails is not the fault of the actual verse, but sometimes, our interpretation of it. So many people will often look at this and then point to how it's a "lie" because they cannot run faster than a car, or perform some other impossible feat. This is not the lesson the verse is trying to teach. It is saying something that most of us refuse to acknowledge. The verse is saying that all things that are possible can be done through Him.

What does this mean exactly? How many times have we said, "I can't"? If we are honest with ourselves, many of us have probably said this before without actually trying. We look at our schedules and think that we can't fit in any more work, or we look at our days and think that we are too exhausted to be able to overcome the trials that are ahead of us, or we simply look at an obstacle and because we've never attempted to before, we almost automatically mark it as an impossibility. These are the concepts that the verse is covering. It is not saying that God will grant you the ability to fly, so much as He will grant you the ability to stand when it seems impossible.

When this verse was written, Paul, the author of Philippians, was in prison. This is not the prison we think of today. There were no laws to protect prisoners once they were inside the cell, there was no reason to feed them three square meals a day. If you were sent to prison, you were locked up and given minimal attention until your sentence had been fulfilled. For someone to write that they can "do all things," we have to think about the context of what that actually means. For someone to be able to write with a sense of positivity when they were surrounded by a world of negativity is something encouraging in itself. It is because of all of this that there is a word that deserves focus in the verse: *able*. With Christ, we are able to make it through all things because it is through Him that we find strength. We are able to take on the negativity of this world because we serve the ultimate positivity.

So whenever you are bogged down with work, or having issues with family, or just trying to fit everything into the day, know this. You are able to do all of these things because it is through Christ that you are given strength!

Thank you for giving me strength, Lord. Continue to be with me during these tough times. Continue to keep me strong.

26

Allow Yourself to Be Challenged

Iron sharpens iron, and one person sharpens another.
PROVERBS 27:17

⌒

There is nothing better and worse than a challenge. Few of us ever like to be challenged at the moment. Even those of us that enjoy a good challenge are more concerned with the aftermath of the challenge than the actual challenge itself. For instance, we typically cannot wait for the challenge to be over because it means that we don't necessarily have to face the challenge any longer. It means that we are able to take a break, that we are able to catch our breath. We should, however, look to a challenge with thankfulness more than simply its ending. We should have gratitude for the strength and experience that comes from a good challenge. Think of a sport you once played or continue to play today. Even though we've seen and heard coaches disciplining their athletes, we've never questioned whether or not the coach cares about his players. Oftentimes, they do this by yelling because they want them to be better. They want to see them become stronger as athletes and as people. It's one of the many reasons that most parents agree that the best thing that you can do for your child is getting them involved in some kind of sport. No matter what the sport is, there is generally a bettering of the athlete on more than just the physical level.

This goes back to us in how we look at challenges. We need to look at challenges with a sense of excitement and gratitude. This is not to say that we cannot acknowledge the difficulties of the mountain in front of us. We are definitely allowed to point out that a challenge is going to be hard, but we need to note that on the other side of this challenge are qualities that are worth going through the challenge in the first place. We look down from a climb with confidence knowing that we made it to the top. We look at the end of a season with gratitude, knowing that we were strong enough to make it through that entire season. We are able to stand on the scale with joy, knowing that every day of hard breathing and profuse sweating had been worth it after all. We look up to that degree hanging on the wall, knowing that the hours and hours of study had been worth it in the long run. Whenever challenges pop up in our lives, we rarely focus on what waits for us in the end. When you have someone trying to make you better through a challenge, instead of trying to fixate on the negativity of the challenge, try and look at it with a grateful spirit. People rarely challenge those in whom they don't find some form of potential for greatness.

Allow me to take on the challenges that are thrown at me. Allow me to look at these challenges with a heart of determination and gratitude, for I know these challenges will only make me stronger.

27

You Are Wonderfully Made

I will praise you because I have been
remarkably and wonderfully made. Your
works are wondrous, and I know this very well.
PSALM 139:14

There are so many days that we wake up and look in the mirror and feel that we are anything but wonderful. Our hair is a mess. Our face needs to be cleaned. Maybe, we even realize that we need to lose a couple of pounds. It is a frustrating sentiment to feel that we are not beautiful, especially when we open our phones and find our social media flooded with pictures of people that we feel are just naturally beautiful, or they seem to have it all figured out. Sometimes the morning mirror can sap away any confidence that we had when we went to bed, or sometimes we go into work and we find out that we haven't done an assignment or project just the way the boss wanted. This is especially frustrating when you look around the office and feel that everyone is having a tremendous day and you are simply trying to crawl your way to the afternoon when you get to go home. Sometimes, we even have an argument with a loved one that makes us feel like we don't have any concept of worth. This is not what God wanted for us. Why? Because He made us. Why would God make anything that He did not plan to be remarkable or wonderful?

Whenever we think on all that has happened in our lives, it is hard some days for us to think that we are anything close to wonderful, but the fact is that you very much are. You were created by the God that created all that is beautiful and good. We all have a bad day from time to time. No one, on this planet, is immune to failure. There are going to be days that you do well, and there are going to be days that you, well, don't. This does not mean that you are not remarkable. This does not mean that you are not incredible or wonderful. We were all created to do amazing things because we were created in the image of the almighty God. When we take this into account, we become incredibly aware of the fact that God would not create something that was incapable of displaying His glory. You were created by the God that made galaxies, stars, planets, oceans, mountains, sunrises, and sunsets. You were created by greatness, and it is through God that you are called to show that greatness to the world. When you think about who had a hand in creating you, how can you be meant to be anything less than wonderful?

Lord, remind me daily that I am loved. Allow me to look
at all that You have created me to be and respond with joy.
I know that You made me to be wonderful and for that,
I thank You for spending the time You did on me.

28

Allow Hope to Anchor You

We have this hope as an anchor for our soul, firm and secure.
It enters the inner sanctuary behind the curtain.
HEBREWS 6:19

⁓

Many people have looked at an anchor as a negative thing. They look at it as something that drags you down and keeps you from moving. If it is something so negative, then why is it one of the most crucial parts of the ship? Anchor chains are often two and a half times longer than the actual vessel itself. It is the part of the ship that is the final guarantee of safety if the engines ever give out and the boat is simply floating aimlessly in the open sea. It is what keeps the ship secure at port—keeping it from floating away in the current of the water. The fact is that anchoring oneself is an acknowledgment of standing firm. It is what keeps us secure. It is because of this that we should view our faith as an anchor.

Why is this so important? There are many storms in life. Some of us will have to deal with sickness. Some of us will have to deal with the loss of a loved one or the loss of a job. Some of us may have to deal with leading a rebellious child. All of these are storms that we will have to face from time to time. One of the things that grounds and anchors us is the notion of our faith. Things seem to be much more manageable when you are aware that you will not be moved. When you feel secure, there is a peace that accompanies the frustrations of life. There will be many times that we will be tossed about in ways that make us terribly uncomfortable, but when we are anchored in our faith, it can make all of the difference in the world. We can take on the obstacles in front of us without worrying about our footing. This is not to say that the obstacles in life are not going to be difficult, but these obstacles are always a little easier to be dealt with when we know that we are secure. We wouldn't try to take a stand for something when we don't trust the ground we are standing on, the same way we won't fair well in a storm when we do not feel secure. Whenever the negativity of this world seems to bog us down, we can respond with strength for we know exactly where that hope is found. Allow your faith to carry you through the storms. Allow your faith to be an anchor in your life that allows you to take on the storms without being tossed overboard. Some storms are so powerful that a ship will go without the anchor, but one's faith is an anchor that can never be overtaken by any storm.

Lord, allow me to continue to have faith in You.
Allow me to be able to look to You with trust in knowing
that I will make it through the tough times in life.

29

𝒩ever 𝐵e 𝒜fraid to 𝓛augh

Strength and honor are her clothing,
and she can laugh at the time to come.
<small>PROVERBS 31:25</small>

There was once a woman that had been diagnosed with cancer. It was one of the scariest times for her family, and yet, she greeted it with a smile. She was scared, of course, but she never allowed her family to see her that way. She would not even allow other patients to see her that way. She was notorious for greeting her family and other patients with a smile and laughter that would lift the spirits of those that were walking through the healing process. When asked about her positive outlook on such a dark time, her response was simple, "I'd rather focus on the healing, than focus on the sickness." She was found cancer-free and officially cured a few years later. What is remarkable is that her family learned to laugh with her during her time of healing. Some of them will say that her laughter is simply that contagious, but others will admit that it was more than that. They will say that it was because of her faith in the doctors and in God that allowed her to laugh in this depressing season, and it was through that faith that they were able to find laughter as well. There were tough days, definitely, but she was always able to put on a smile and laugh for her family and for her outlook on the future. It was something that showed her strength and dignity to be able to look in the face of illness and smile.

What does this story tell us about our lives today? How often are we driven to frustration and sadness because of the little things in life? Why do we not allow ourselves to laugh whenever times seem tougher than normal? The fact is that in all times, even in the hard ones, we are called to live a life of positivity. We are not called to allow ourselves to be pulled down by the negativity in life. We are not called to fall into depression in the trials that come our way. We are called to respond in all things with a sense of positivity and laughter, but above all, we must be able to respond with dignity. We have to be willing to show that no worldly frustration or obstacle will ever be strong enough to overtake the power of God. It is because of this knowledge that we have to be willing to respond to the negative situations in life with a sense of positivity. We have to hold onto our sense of joy, even in the moments of the unknown. It is in this positivity that we show a sense of strength and a sense of honor, and it is only within those that we can ever feel strong enough to laugh.

Remind me daily of the strength and honor that
You have given me. Remind me to laugh, even in the
moments that seem too difficult to find laughter.

30

Don't Underestimate Your Faith

*"Because of your little faith," he told them. "For truly
I tell you, if you have faith the size of a mustard seed,
you will tell this mountain, 'Move from here to there,'
and it will move. Nothing will be impossible for you."*

MATTHEW 17:20

~

Have you ever seen a mustard plant? A small one is about as tall as the average man, and the largest ones can grow up to around thirty feet or higher if they are tended properly and fare well under ideal conditions. They are absolutely one of the most interesting plants simply because of their origins. A mustard seed is not even one-tenth of an inch. It is an incredibly small seed. If dropped in the soil, the untrained eye would definitely lose track of where it fell. It can sit on the tip of the finger and almost be mistaken for a speck of dirt. It is one of the smallest seeds known to man that can be seen by the naked eye, and yet produces some of the tallest crops that we continue to harvest today.

Now, Jesus did not mean this verse literally. He did not literally mean that with faith we can walk up to a mountain and say move, and it will do so. Many have tried to prove how the verse is wrong, which honestly shows their lack of faith in the first place, but I digress. The point is this, those who have faith normally can do just about anything.

Henry Ford once said, "Whether you think you can, or you think you can't—you're right." There is a lot of truth to this in regards to faith. How many of us have walked up on a situation and automatically assumed that it can't be done? Many have looked at the impossible throughout history and then turned it into the ordinary. Many have invented different things that have added to our society in tremendous ways simply because they believed that it could be done. Look at the world you live in, and think back as far as you can. How much exists today because someone said it could in the first place?

With faith, nothing is impossible for us because with faith comes a sense of knowing what is possible. It is not a hope. It is more than that. A hope is what we use to describe a concept that might happen. Faith is a belief that something will happen. That is why Christ used the mustard seed as His main comparison to faith. Think about someone that does not know what a mustard seed can become. They will look at that tiny speck on your fingertip and assume that nothing will come of it. They may surmise that only a few inches of green will come from the seed, but we know what comes from taking care of that seed. We know that the harvest is unfathomably large.

Lord, thank You for my faith. Allow me to foster
that faith and tend it so all the things that may
come will not be impossible for me to handle.

31

He Knows Our Hurt

*I will rejoice and be glad in your faithful love because you have
seen my affliction. You have known the troubles of my soul.*
PSALM 31:7

~

Something most of us have probably heard from other loved ones is the
tearful sentence said in response to our trying to care, "You wouldn't
understand!" It is one of the hardest things for us to hear. It is something that
hurts us to our core because sometimes, as much as we hate to admit it, it's
true. Some of us will go through a hurt that few will ever understand. Some
of us will struggle in ways that others may never have to go through. There,
however, is a light in this dark situation that many of us often forget. That truth
is this. Even though the rest of the world may never have any kind of inkling as
to what you are going through, God knows the troubles of your life. He knows
what plagues your soul, and it is in that we can find comfort.

Frankly, there is nothing better than finding someone that knows your
pain. Whenever we find someone that knows the path we are walking because
they have been down the road before us, there is a move, ever so slightly, to
joy. You find that within this war you've been fighting alone, you have somehow found a comrade. No matter how difficult the journey has been, there is
now someone that you're overjoyed to speak with because you know that they
understand you and your struggles. You almost feel like the love that these

people show you is more genuine because they understand what it takes to look past your struggles and love you for who you are.

We often forget that even though these people have loved you on a level that you greatly appreciate, their love is nothing compared to the level of love God has for you simply because of the fact that God knows you through and through. God knows you at your highest and God knows you at your lowest, and He loves you know matter which stage you currently find yourself. Unlike the highs and lows of our life, God's love never changes. It is constant.

There is something incredible about the constant love of God. Most of us have probably come to learn in one form or another that God loves us in spite of ourselves. He loves us when it is not easy for us to be loved, and God loves us through our troubles. It does not even matter whether or not those troubles were caused by our own doing, what matters is that God's love is still faithful even in the midst of knowing our troubles. How can we not rejoice in God when He loves us more than anyone ever could in moments when anyone hardly would?

Thank You for loving me in the times when I am in trouble. Thank You for easing my soul in times when it feels as if it cannot be soothed.

32

Let Go of Your Complaints

If I said, "I will forget my complaint,
change my expression, and smile."
JOB 9:27

~

There is something to be said about looking on the brighter side. We all know how important it is to be optimistic and yet, so few of us ever try to do just that. We live in a half-full world, but we are always so prone to viewing it as half-empty when the world throws a frustration or two in our midst.

For instance, we may look in a mirror and find a face that many say is beautiful, but for some reason when we see it, it only takes one single, solitary blemish to make that face look as if it's not worth viewing at all. Some of us will then take a look at our cars that have gotten us from point A to point B for as long as we can remember, but the moment we have to do anything more than an oil change, we wonder why we got the car in the first place. Maybe we'll even find ourselves in a new job. We were excited about the job when we first got there. It definitely seemed better than the last one, but the moment something pops up about the job that doesn't seem to fit well with your expectations, we think that there is something wrong with the job altogether. What do we do during these times of frustration? If we're honest with ourselves, we probably spend a few moments, probably more, complaining. We use the time given to us to speak pessimistically about our current situations instead of taking a moment to point out the good in what we do, or at least try and figure out how to fix the problem that is standing in front of us.

For most of us, we have probably come to know, or have been, two different kinds of people in the moments of frustration. There is the one that the majority of the world falls into, the pessimists, and the other one where the rest fall into, the optimists. The difference between the two all centers around the concept of attitude. Frustrations and obstacles are going to come. It is a part of life. What matters is how we handle those frustrations. There are many of us that do not know how to deal with all of the issues that fall upon us. Many of us put on a veil of defeat and assume that the world is out to get us, but a few of us are different. A few of us will look at the problem, take in a deep breath, smile, and say, "How do we fix it?" These are the kind of people that move positively through the world. Be like these people. Forget about your complaint, smile, and move forward with God.

> Father, I'm sorry for the times that I've held onto
> negativity. Remind me to let go of that negativity
> and take on these obstacles with a smile.

33

Be Glad in His Day

This is the day the LORD has made;
let us rejoice and be glad in it.
PSALM 118:24

~

Every now and again the Bible will give us the perfect greeting for the morning after we rise from the bed. Some of us who have early commutes have a difficult time trying to find this gladness, but it is there if we simply look for it. One of the things that has changed the lives of some people is waking up about thirty minutes before they actually have to be out of bed for their morning routines. In doing this, they take the time to step outside and observe the early morning world. There are birds beginning to chirp. The ground is wet from dew. We see the faint glow of the sun rising in the distance. We feel the cool air start to leave as the sun starts to heat our portion of the earth. All of these things have something in common. All of these are tiny markers of the early morning world that begin to prepare the earth for signs of life. Hours before you rise, the world is asleep and because of God's love, He allows it to wake. He provides sunlight to eliminate the darkness. He provides water without rain to feed the plants. He stirs animals and brings life. He gives us that deep breath of air we take in each morning before we sit up to take on the day. It is through the love of God that we are able to stand and look out to another day in which He has made.

How can we not rejoice in that? How can we not take in the new day that God has allowed us to see and not find joy in all that He has done? He has done more than just prepare the world for life. He has gone above and beyond in ways that we cannot fathom. He has kept the planet in orbit around a star that gives us just enough heat to sustain life. He has provided us with an atmosphere that is able to give us the proper conditions to give us the ability to live. There are so many scientific parts to our daily existence that would cause a constant rejoicing if we were able to comprehend all of the millions of things that God allows to happen that give us life.

The final reason for rejoicing is one that is simple. It is us. God kept our hearts beating throughout the night. He continued to give air that would fill our lungs. He gave us a mind that sends signals to the rest of the body that it is time for us to rise. We cannot even begin to fathom this, but it is through God's constant and innumerable forms of love that we are even able to observe the day that He is made. How can we not rejoice when we have this knowledge?

Father, thank You for the day. Allow me to constantly
rejoice in the day that You have made.

34

God Is Wherever We Are

*"Haven't I commanded you: be strong and
courageous? Do not be afraid or discouraged,
for the LORD your God is with you wherever you go."*
JOSHUA 1:9

It is always an unsettling feeling, to say the least, that we would ever be put in a predicament alone. We live in a world where we are constantly cautioned about the dangers of being alone. We are told that wherever we go, we should do our best to never go on our own. There is so much truth to this. The world, sadly, is a scary place. Whenever you travel, it is always explained that you should not be by yourself. Whenever we go out with friends, we are normally told to stay together until it is safe to be alone. When we live in a world where the messages tell us that there are things in the world that are out to get us, it holds the danger of making us afraid of the world we live in. We can often end up becoming a people that are frightened by every little thing that could or could not potentially be waiting for us in the shadows.

How can we live in a world like this? How can we hope to thrive in a place where we are essentially told that we should live in constant fear? The fact of the matter is that we were not called to be a fearful people. We were never designed to be people that were afraid of anything. We were commanded to be strong and courageous everywhere we go because of the fact that God is with us wherever we go.

Look at those that have been courageous before us. Figures like David were not fearless on their own merit. He was not courageous because he instinctively had a gene in him that made him have more courage than the average man. He was courageous because of the fact that he had faith that God was with him. Through this courage, David defeated giants, he led armies, and he governed a kingdom. David was courageous, yes, but it was not because of any quality that he possessed on his own. It was because he knew that God was with him.

The same can be said in our lives. Many of us lead families, conquer the obstacles in our jobs, and guide others with wisdom. These are responsibilities that most would respond with cowardice, and yet, we cannot put ourselves in this emotion. We have to be willing to stand. We have to be willing to move forward. We have to be strong and courageous. This is something that gets easier each day because of the fact that we are not alone. Our courageous spirits and strong wills are simply by-products that come from our unrelenting faith in a God that never leaves our side.

Lord, thank You for being with me. Continue to stand with me and give me strength and courage to take on all that lies before me.

35

May His Face Shine on You

"May the LORD make his face shine on you and be gracious to you."
NUMBERS 6:25

~

There is nothing better than receiving a blessing. As the frustrations of this world seem to close in on us from every angle, a blessing can make all the difference. So many of us, however, will often forget to acknowledge all of the blessings that we have received. So many of us will not even become aware that God's face is shining on our lives. There is a lot to be said about the thankfulness one can and should have over the blessings received from God.

Many of us, if we're honest, can probably think of a blessing that we have received each day. It may have been a form that provides, or a form that protects, or a form that sustains. Whatever it may be, God has shined on our lives even in the hard days. Think about it. How often do we go about our lives and seemingly dodge the pitfalls that could have made the day worse? How often do we take on moments of failure and yet, have somehow avoided the issues that would have made it worse? Even better, how many of us have seemed to sidestep the negativity of life altogether? How many of us had the opportunity to just take on a good day? There are so many different moments in life where it is obvious that God loves us, and in that love, He blesses our lives.

Think about your day so far. If it's in the morning, you have somehow been granted the ability to find time to learn a little bit more about God. You might have all of these little things to take care of, and yet, God has blessed you with the opportunity and time to take time to spend time with just you and Him. Maybe you're reading this in the afternoon or evening. God has blessed you in making it to the end of the day. He's blessed you with protection in making it home safely. He's given you the ability to make it through the day without any major complications on your life. He's allowed the chaos of the day to settle so that you can find rest in your time with Him.

Some of you, however, may not feel this way. Some of you may be reading this and thinking, *My day has been terrible.* Even if this is how you feel, you still sought out time to be with God. Even in the form of this book, you were able to sit and be with Him. God carried you, or is even still carrying you, through the pitfalls of this season and has blessed you with the strength to still seek Him out in this time of frustration.

As much as we hate to admit it, our relationship with God is one that is a blessing in itself. No matter how good or bad the day may be, God blesses us by loving us.

Thank You for loving me, Lord. Thank You for blessing me with Your love. Allow me to take this blessing with gratitude and graciousness.

36

The State of Your Heart

A joyful heart makes a face cheerful,
but a sad heart produces a broken spirit.
PROVERBS 15:13

⁓

We can always tell when someone is having a good day. We can always tell when someone has a joyful heart. It shows when they are able to come into work on a Monday with a smile on their face. It shows when they are able to smile in the face of adversity. It shows when a challenge is something that is accepted.

It also shows when someone is in possession of a sad heart. There is a brokenness to them. They seem tired. They seem as if the world is against them. There is a sense of defeat in all of the things that they do. It is one of the hardest things to watch if you care for this person, and one of the first actions we take to love on this person is to drag their sad heart into a place of joy. The point is this, that the heart determines the ways of our spirit, and it shows to the rest of the world.

There are many moments where the world will try to break us. Maybe you have had to be late for work for the third time in one week. Maybe you are dealing with the heartache of loss. Maybe the obstacles of the day seem to be something that you just can't seem to overcome. Whatever the reason, if you allow the negativity of the world to seep into your heart, it will be evident to everyone else. No matter the amount of effort you may place in hiding the heartache from others, the people that care will be able to tell that something is not quite right.

When the world is right, however, it is one of the most joyous feelings in the world. People gravitate toward you. They are drawn in by your confidence and joy. People automatically want to know what is going on in your life that has affected you in such a positive way. Whatever the reason, your heart is a signal to the rest of the world in how you are feeling. No matter how talented we may be at hiding our emotions from others, the ones that love us can always seem to tell when something in our lives is filling us with joy or brokenness.

This, in itself, is a notion that should fill us with joy. God gave us hearts that so easily show our emotions. God allows our hearts to do the talking for us. He allows us to show the world that there are times of brokenness when we need help, even if we are not willing to ask for it. It is also incredible that God has given our hearts the same ability to show the world when we are in a season of joy. No matter what our hearts show, however, there is an automatic glorification of God. When we are in a season of despair, our hearts show how much we need Him, and when they show joy, our hearts show how much we love Him.

Father, thank You for my heart. Thank You for allowing
to show others when I am in a season of need and
in a season of joy. Allow me to use it to constantly glorify You.

37

Happiness in Blessings from God

Happy are the people with such blessings.
Happy are the people whose God is the LORD.
PSALM 144:15

~

We have all seen them; the kind of people that never seem to be satisfied. They are the kind of people that seem to have everything that they could ever desire and somehow, they seem to want more. The car that seems brand-new to some is not up to the standard of the owner. The home that seems beautiful to some eyes, might be something that "needs a lot of love" for the owner. The job that pays well and has flexible hours according to the eyes of those looking at the job from the outside will often be confronted with the employee working that job—saying they hate their career. We have all heard the sentiment that the grass is always greener on the other side of the fence, but it does not change the fact that your grass is still green. Some of us are too occupied with our own dissatisfaction that we cannot seem to find the happiness in the blessings that we've already received.

It seems like a pretty self-explanatory notion to say that we should happy because God blesses us. We should have a level of happiness over all the things that God had done in our lives, but those blessings are sometimes the things that we are all so guilty of overlooking. So many of us have definitely been blessed immensely, and for some reason or another, people would not be able to tell based on our behavior surrounded by those blessings. There is an attitude that comes with our relationship with God and the blessings that He provides us, and that attitude should be one that is reflective of our happiness with Him.

Look at your life. Look at all of the things that God has done and you may just realize a few of the blessing that God has given you. He's given you breath in your lungs, a heart that beats, family and friends that love and care for you. You have love. You have a God that cares for you on a level that others will never come close to understanding. We serve a God that loves us to the point at which He gave His only Son for us so that we might live. No matter the level of blessings in your life, you cannot escape the fact that God loves us so much that He blessed us by changing the fate of our eternity by giving us His Son on the cross. When we realize that this is the God we serve and these are the blessings that He gives, we can only respond with a spirit that is grateful and filled with an overwhelming joy.

Father, thank You for blessing us. Thank You for showering
my life with the various blessings that You have given.
Allow me to respond to these blessings with joy.

38

Joy Came with a Price

Keeping our eyes on Jesus, the source and
perfecter of our faith. For the joy that lay before him,
he endured a cross, despising the shame, and sat
down at the right hand of the throne of God.
HEBREWS 12:2

One of the most difficult things for us to realize is that Christ gave us joy in our freedom from death. We have heard that freedom comes with a price. It is one of the things that many of us have seen written or heard since we were young. The price was something that we could never hope to pay. It was a price that we were unable to pay. No amount of work would ever be enough to bring us to a place where we might be able to even come close.

There was a joy that Christ was aware of on the other side of the cross. He knew that on the other side of the cross was the promise of heaven and eternal joy with God. Jesus was fully knowledgeable of what it was going to take for humanity to be able to be saved. The payment for this joy was going to be Christ's enduring of the cross. He would have to spend hours in a state of torturous pain—being mocked by the people that He had come to save. We cannot even begin to imagine the level of pain caused by the physical ailments that were placed upon Him as well as the cutting embarrassment that came from the ones who had rejected Him. On the other side of the cross, however, Christ brought victory and joy in what had been done.

It is through Christ that our faith is found perfect in the eyes of God. Through the sacrifice of Christ, we were able to be found blameless before God. It is a concept that we can never even begin to understand, but it is a notion that we have all been able to receive great joy. Christ knew that it was only through His sacrifice on the cross that this joy was going to be possible. He knew that dying an agonizing death—a death filled with pain, chastisement, and rejection—was going to be the only way that we would ever be able to receive the joy that was on the other side of that cross.

How do we respond to this? How do we take in what has happened through Christ's death and respond appropriately to that sacrifice? The response is a simple one. We are to respond with joy. Some of us may think that this freedom from death is one that comes with a price, or it is something that we are unworthy of receiving, and the fact is that they are right. That, however, is not how gifts work. Gifts are given out of love with the purpose in mind to bring joy. Christ gave a gift with an eternal benefit with a joy that is unparalleled and will never be matched.

Jesus, thank You for giving me the gift that I don't deserve. Thank You for loving me enough to give me the gift of perfect faith and eternal joy.

39

Dwell on the Good in Life

Finally brothers and sisters, whatever is true,
whatever is honorable, whatever is just,
whatever is pure, whatever is lovely,
whatever is commendable—if there is any
moral excellence and if there is anything
praiseworthy—dwell on these things.
PHILIPPIANS 4:8

⁓

Sometimes it can feel like we are surrounded by the bad in the world. We can almost feel as if there is no way of escaping it when, in reality, it may just be a simple thing as adjusting our perspective. We may need to change what it is that holds our focus.

How does this happen? Well, the first thing that we may have to realize is that we may not be able to actually change the problem. There are some things that we will never be able to fix, and that is not necessarily a bad thing. Maybe we were never meant to fix the problem at hand, but if it can't be fixed at the moment, then why are we giving it so much power over our lives? Why are we allowing something that is negatively affecting us to be able to reside in our lives? The answer is simple. We have to change our hearts' residence. We have to be willing to dwell on the good in life.

How do we do this? It is not as if we can simply create good in the times that are bad. Maybe we are not able to make good out of the bad. The fact is that there is always an opportunity to have a focus on what is good. We have an opportunity to focus on the truth of the matter. The Bible is filled with truths that point to the light in the darkness, that point to the notion of finding the positive in the negative. We know that we are loved by God and that He is always with us. Even in the bad times, hold onto this truth.

For what is honorable, that is found in our action. Whenever you find yourself in a time of frustration, meditate on how the honorable would respond to the frustration. Do not allow yourself to succumb to the temptation of lashing out selfishly. Instead, choose to respond with honor.

When we focus on the just and the pure, we will often notice the wrong in the world. This is not an invitation to a crusade, but it is an invitation to focus on what is right in the world. There are plenty of moments that may seem unjust or impure; focus on how to make it right instead of focussing on its destruction.

For what is lovely and commendable, these can be centered around our response to the world. Be someone that people love and respect. Think about what you love and respect and take on those characteristics and share them with the world around you.

All of these concepts center around the concept of morality. No matter how you may feel in all that you do, choose the moral. You may just be surprised that the level of joy that comes over choosing morality instead of selfishness.

Lord, thank You for all of the things that are right in this world. Remind me to make these things my focus. Remind me to constantly chase after what is good in your eyes.

40

Find Rest in Him

"Come to me, all of you who are weary
and burdened, and I will give you rest."
MATTHEW 11:28

~

There are many things in this life that will just wear us down. We are burdened by so many different things. Some of us deal with jobs that drain us. Some of us have to take care of children that constantly need more and more attention. Some of us have long commutes that seem to deplete our energy before we ever even make it to the office building. There are so many different things that constantly make our hearts yearn for a place to rest. So few people know the level of rest we can find in Christ.

Many people don't realize this, but the job of a working mother is one of the most difficult professions you could ever have. Alison has three boys and will tell you that it is no walk in the park. She gets up at four o'clock in the morning every single day. She spends time in prayer and the Word before she does anything else. At five, she closes her Bible and gets to work on the boy's breakfast while making their lunches. It is something that has become an art after years of practice. Even though there were definitely a few times where she served the boys ham sandwiches for breakfast and sent them off with cereal for lunch. After she sends the boys off to go wait for the bus, she does some early morning cleaning and then leaves for work at six thirty. She sits in traffic for an hour, then works from eight to three and leaves to get home to start on dinner. The boys get home, and dinner is served at five thirty. After dinner, she spends time with her husband and they go on their evening run together. She then comes home, takes a shower, and does laundry and spends another ten to fifteen minutes in the Word just to wake up and do it all again tomorrow.

Something you will notice about Alison, however, is that she never seems to be that worn down. She's definitely tired, but she never really allows herself to be overcome by the wearing down caused each day. Whenever other parents ask her how she does it, she simply responds with this, "Each day is hard, but I take special care to start and end my time the same way. I always do my best to start my day with God and end it with Him as well."

So many of us allow ourselves to get sucked into the rhythm of our day-to-day without actually taking time to stop and meditate on our time with God. Take time to reach out to Him each day. Resting in Him is one of the greatest pauses in the day that we could ever need.

Lord, remind me each day to put my trust in You.
Remind me that you are the one that gives rest and that it is
You that provides strength in a world that tries to weaken me.

41

We Are Never Satisfied on Our Own

Sheol and Abaddon are never satisfied,
and people's eyes are never satisfied.
PROVERBS 27:20

~

We live in a world of want. We live in a world that tells you to climb the ladder, that tells you life is all-you-can-eat, that tells you to make more and more money. Our world seems to be one that is never satisfied. Many of us have heard this sentiment before, that "our eyes are bigger than our stomachs." There is a great deal of truth to this, but I think that it can go a step further: our eyes are greater than our needs.

Think about this for a moment. What are the times that we eat the most? For many of us, we would probably admit that a good portion of our heavy eating takes place during the holiday season. Between Thanksgiving and Christmas, there is a reason why most New Year's resolutions center around the notion of losing weight. I want you, however, to specifically think about the food at the family table. Each member has brought something to add to the food that is prepared. There are desserts of many different kinds, enough meat to feed a family twice, a few vegetables from the health nut in the family, and the different sides that only complement the meal. There is no way that we need all of the food that is present, and yet, how many of us take on the challenge of having some of all of it? Our eyes are never satisfied with our needs.

This is not just on the basis of food. Some of us know someone that puts hours and hours into their work to get that next pay raise or the next promotion. Whenever that day comes, instead of taking a moment to notice all they have accomplished, they normally press their nose closer to the grindstone—focusing on the next phase in their career.

Some of us know the materialist. They have the nicest odds and ends that anyone could ever want. They have the newest model car, the biggest house in the neighborhood, and the fancy clothes. Do they ever stop with this materialism? Is there ever a time when they reach a sense of satisfaction? Of course not. Their eyes are always on the future so that they can update their belongings as those updates come into their view.

This is not what God wanted for us. The eyes of man can be satisfied when they simply maintain a focus on that which will give ultimate satisfaction. Think about the people that are happiest in your life. They are not necessarily known for the status or their belongings. They are known for their passions. When we are fulfilled in our identity, our souls are satisfied, that is something our eyes cannot alter. Keep your eyes on Christ and find a spirit that is fulfilled and satisfied.

Lord, remind me to keep my eyes on You. Allow me to seek after you and find satisfaction in all that You do for me.

42

God Can Be Trusted Forever

Trust in the LORD forever, because in the LORD,
the LORD himself, is an everlasting rock!
ISAIAH 26:4

⁓

How many of us have ever been let down? Most of us, if not all of us, can probably point to a time where someone let us down immensely. Even people we love have disappointed us from time to time. Some of us might even say that we had lost our faith in some of these people. Trust is something that we only reserve for those that we deem worthy of that trust. There is an unofficial, unwritten list of qualification that each person needs in order to be one of the few that we can ever trust. Even with these intensive qualifications, each and every person that we would consider trustworthy has probably done something that is undeserving of that trust.

Whenever we deal with the notion of trust, there is a lot that goes into its definition. What does it mean to trust someone? To trust someone means that there is a reliance on the outcome of a behavior that you have grown to know. For instance, we can trust someone who has proven to be a good listener to listen to us whenever we have a problem. We can probably also trust that a career criminal will probably turn back to a life of crime after they get out of prison. We can trust in good behavior, but we can also trust in a bad one. The kind of trust that we seek, however, is the kind that shows we can rely on someone. The trust we need is to know that this someone will be there for us in our time of need. As sad as it is to say, there is no one on this planet that will ever be able to be perfectly trustworthy. Whether we like it or not, even the most trustworthy person we know has done something that would not be considered worthy of trust.

Whenever we think about the kind of trust that we are after, we immediately try and seek out the trust that will be everlasting. That is why we have vows at weddings. We do our best to allow our spouse to know that we will promise to love and respect them until death. A vow is as close as we can get to everlasting trust, and even then, there will be times that we hear about a divorce.

With God, however, many of us have probably come to know that He provides a trust that is everlasting. We can trust in God forever, because He, Himself, is everlasting. There is a reason that He is described as an everlasting rock. A rock is about as close as we can get to something lasting forever, and the trust we have in God is one that will even outlast that. Trust in God and find that He is the only one that can ever maintain a trust that is everlasting.

Lord, remind me of Your trustworthiness. Remind me to seek after You in all that I do. Thank You for loving me. Lord, thank You for proving every day that Your love and trust is something that lasts forever.

43

The Righteous Are Glad

But the righteous are glad; they rejoice
before God and celebrate with joy.
PSALM 68:3

~

To start, this is not a way of telling you that people that are always right are always happy. A smug attitude does not equal joy, as some of us have come to know from time to time. There are some of us, however, that have come to know that there is a joy in doing the right thing. It may not be immediate, but it is something that does bring a special dose of happiness to our lives.

It is something that we have been told to do our entire lives. We are told that doing the right thing will end with our happiness. Even though this is something that we have heard multiple times over the years, it continues to be one of the greatest challenges to humanity. Many of us, no matter how often you tell us, don't ever seem to become aware of the joy that waits for those who live a life of integrity.

Most of us can remember a time when we were younger and we were offered the chance to do what is right and still chose to go in a different direction. There was once a boy who knew he was failing a class. The father had suspected that the boy's grades were beginning to suffer. When the father came to his son to see how his class was going, the boy responded with an "Everything is going well." The boy had chosen to lie to his father, and because of that lie, he was robbed of any joy when his report cards came home—revealing that everything was not going as well as it could have. The boy had to deal with two consequences as opposed to just one. The boy had to deal with the punishment of failing a class, but also suffer the disappointment of a father who had been lied to. The next year, the boy was in a similar predicament. The father came to his son once more and asked how his classes were going. This time the boy chose to come clean and admit that there was a problem. The father's response was not anger, but instead, he took the role of a provider and gave his son the help he needed to pass his class. When the report cards came out and revealed that his grades were all above average, the boy could celebrate a joy that was now two-fold. He could celebrate that he had made a good grade, but even more so, he could celebrate honesty with his father over his grades.

Righteousness works in similar ways. When we celebrate all that has happened because of our decisions, we can also take joy in knowing that those decisions were made righteously. Even when we fall, we can still take joy in knowing we did what we thought was right.

Remind me daily what is right. Allow me to have
a focus on what is righteous and instill in me a heart
that desires to act according to that righteousness.

44

Celebrate Good Times Provided by Hard Work

*I know that there is nothing better for them than to
rejoice and enjoy the good life. It is also the gift of God
whenever anyone eats, drinks, and enjoys all his efforts.*
ECCLESIASTES 3:12-13

A florist is one of the worst jobs to have in the summer. It is a time of great business, but it is also the busiest season of the year for one reason: weddings. One florist, in particular, spoke about some of the frustrations of the summer season. There are brides that want flowers that are out of season. They will want flowers that have to be imported, or they will put in an order so large that it would have been cheaper for them just to seek out a venue with a garden. One of the happiest times for the florist, however, is in September. Using her words, she would say "My business is cut by seventy-five percent! No one gets married in September!" She often refers to it as her post-summer vacation.

What does she do with this month? She uses the whole month as a vacation. She goes on trips with her family. Her kids are taken out of school and they all go somewhere for a week. She rests, celebrates, and enjoys the work she has accomplished.

It is the same for us. Whenever we have put in a great deal of work into anything, it is completely appropriate for us to enjoy the fruits of our labor. That fruit looks different for everyone. For some, it may be taking a vacation. For others, it may be something as simple as spending an extra hour relaxing. The point, however, is this: Whenever you have worked hard, it is completely appropriate for us to put our feet up and smile, for our work has paid off.

This celebration is, of course, a gift. It is something that God has given us as a natural response to the work we've done. What we must realize, however, is that there is a certain part to this that most people overlook: the actual work. We cannot take in a deep breath and look out at a field of nothing. We can't just simply celebrate that it is Tuesday and we got out of bed. There has to be a level of work that we have to put in for us to be able to have any form of celebration.

That is what makes whatever we do so special. Whenever we put in a great deal of effort into anything, there is a celebration that follows. It may be one that is grand, or it may be one that is only meant for a few, but whatever the type of celebration, it all comes down to the same concept. Celebration and joy are a natural product of hard work. So go out. Work hard, and celebrate your accomplishments. You've earned it!

Thank You for hard work, Lord. Allow me to continue to
work hard in all that I do. Remind me to celebrate the good
that I have done, and to take that celebration as a gift from You.

45

Pray Effectively

Is anyone among you suffering? He should pray.
Is anyone cheerful? He should sing praises.
JAMES 5:13

~

There is nothing better than prayer. It is the way that all of us have in order to communicate with God. The beautiful part of prayer is that it doesn't matter if we are in a season of suffering or if we are in a season of joy. Prayer is prayer.

No one likes to think about suffering. It is even something that is unpleasant to talk about. It makes us uncomfortable to hear about it. It is even worse when we are in the middle of living through it, but even in our suffering, there is a way for us to be able to reach out to God. Through prayer, we are able to move into a world where God is listening. It is one of the most powerful sentiments to think that when the world has put so much weight on our shoulders that we fall to our knees, we are in the perfect position for prayer. No matter how great the suffering is, God is always ready to listen to and answer our prayers.

On the other side of the spectrum, there are moments with so much joy that we cannot even begin to contain ourselves. Joy is one of the most amazing emotions we can feel because of its power. When we simply think on the source of the joy, we are almost immediately sucked back into the time and place where that joy was first felt. It is in this time that we are able to move from the emotion of joy to the powerful feeling of thanksgiving. It is in this notion of thanksgiving that we can reach up to God and sing His praises.

When we think about the full spectrum of emotions that are covered in between one's joy and one's suffering, we realize something that is very powerful. The realization is that no matter where we are on the spectrum, God is always willing to listen. It does not matter if we are happy, sad, or hungry, a prayer will always be heard. No matter what season you are in or emotion you may feel, you can always respond to such with prayer.

Every single one of us is able to reach out to God every single and day and yet, so few of us ever take the time to do so. No matter what season of life you are currently in, don't miss out on the power of prayer. It is appropriate during our times of hurt and suffering, and it is appropriate during our times of celebration and victory. Whatever the season may be, reach out to God and know that He is listening.

Father, thank You for prayer. Thank You for giving us a way to reach out to You during all seasons. Lord, remind me every day that no matter what season I find myself, I can always reach out to You.

46

Asking for Help Is the First Step

Until now you have asked for nothing in my name. Ask and you will receive, so that your joy may be complete.

JOHN 16:24

❧

There is nothing worse than admitting that you need help. It's almost as if we have to put ourselves in such a place where we have to admit that we don't have it all figured out. No one likes to be in this situation. No one likes finding themselves in a place where they feel unequipped or incomplete. So many of us, however, tend to operate in this fashion every single day. All of us happen to go out into the world and act like everything is just fine, but none of us want to actually admit that we may need a little bit of help.

In many ways, we share the same qualities found in children whenever they are faced with an insurmountable obstacle. They look at the challenge set before them, and as soon as the parent tries to step in and help, the child will often throw a tantrum—demanding that they are able to do whatever needs to be done. Like children, we never want to admit that something is outside of our understanding. We never want to acknowledge that we cannot do something even if it would mean that a solution could be found.

This is not what God wanted for us. God never wanted us to feel as if we were not equipped to handle something. He never wanted us to wander aimlessly with no purpose. God wants us to be able to take on all things that lie before us with confidence. What we have to realize is that in order to find the joy of confidence, we must be willing to ask for help through prayer. This is where it gets a little difficult for some of us. The difficulty lies in admitting that we need help.

Asking for help never seems to be a pleasant venture. It never seems to be something that we really want to do. A lot of this is because of our pride, but asking God for any kind of help means actively letting go of that pride. It also comes with a realization. Asking God for help does come with an answer. That answer, however, may not exactly be what we think it is. When we pray for knowledge or strength, we cannot expect God to simply pour them into our minds and bodies. He is more likely to give us opportunities or people that will help give us answers to our prayers. God will always give us what we pray for, but it is our responsibility to actually receive it. Being made complete is something that requires a little bit of action on our end. God will give us the needs that we request, but we have to be willing to actively receive the answers to those prayers in order to reach a state of complete joy.

Lord, thank You for answering my prayers. Allow me to receive the answers to those prayers so that I may find joy in what You have done.

47

Your Heart Is Worth Protecting

Guard your heart above all else, for it is the source of life.
Proverbs 4:23

⌒

Something most parents have discussed is how to raise their children. One of the greatest debates that have existed within the study of parenthood is the application of the protection of a child's innocence. Psychologists all over the world argue over the different nuances of thought on the subject. Some say that controlled exposure is the best form available. Some say that we should expose children to as much of the world as appropriate while others would say that children should have as much shelter as possible for as long as possible. Wherever one falls on this spectrum of thought, they have to acknowledge that all of this discussion is centered around the concept of protecting a child's heart. The heart is a very precious thing. It is something that deserves to be guarded.

Children are not the only ones that can benefit from this line of thought. Many of us could probably take the time to guard our own hearts as well. There are so many heartbreaking things about this world when we actually take the time to ponder on the implications of the world. We find humor in chaos. We glue ourselves to television shows that tell stories of unnecessary drama and heartache. We stand in line for movies that fill us with fear. We get wrapped up in the gossip at work. We pay large amounts of money to watch people beat each other to pulps. Frankly put, we have trained our hearts to seek out the chaos in this world. This is not what our hearts were designed to seek. They were designed to seek what is good.

Think about all of the memories that we hold dear. They normally are centered around the concept of goodness. We remember birthday parties, family reunions, graduations. We remember the moments of laughter and joy with loved ones. We remember the first times we met friends that have grown to mean the world to us. We have hearts that naturally desire the good in this life. Like our bodies, our heart is at its best when we are giving it what is good for it, but like our bodies, our hearts ache whenever we push that which is bad for it into it.

It is because of all of this that our heart is so precious. Our hearts seek what is good. It should never be exposed to the bad, and yet, so many of us expose our hearts to the negativity of the world. Look at your life. Is there anything in your life that is seeping into your heart that shouldn't? Is your heart not precious? Does it not deserve protection from the bad in the world?

Allow me to look at my heart, Lord. Allow me to realize
the good that is in my life that my heart needs to see,
and allow me to avoid the negative.

48

Making Peace Brings Light

Blessed are the peacemakers,
for they will be called sons of God.
MATTHEW 5:9

~

Think about high school. For some of us, high school was not the most pleasant of memories. For others, we wish that we could relive them. Some may even be living through it now. There are many things that have changed about high school over the years. There are more sports available. There is a club for everything and everyone, but even though there have been all of these changes, there has been one thing that has never changed: bullies. No matter the high school experience, all of them can point out to which one was the bully of the school.

Even though high school may have been, or may still be, a tumultuous time for some of us. Most of us can always remember the rarest member of the high school: the peacemaker. This person was one of the most appreciated members of the student body. They were liked by most, if not all, of the school faculty, and were respected by the vast majority of the student body. The reason for this attitude toward the peacemaker was a simple one. People were able to recognize that this person only cared about keeping the peace.

For those of us that remember high school, it is one of the most selfish periods during the adolescent years. This is selfishness is caused by the encouragement of self-centeredness in the teen years. Questions like, "Where do you want to go to college?" or "What do you want to be when you get older?" constantly sprinkle the environment when you are a teen. Teenagers get asked everything about themselves from their present to their future. It is only natural that high school is a time when we see teenagers think about themselves. Peacemakers, however, are different. They are normally thinking about others.

Some of us may not know what a peacemaker exactly is, but when we discuss it, it becomes obvious as to who the peacemaker is in our school. A peacemaker is normally seen helping. You see someone's books fall to the floor and the peacemaker is the one that helps collect them. You see someone being bullied, and the peacemaker is normally the one that gets involved to stop it. Simply put, a peacemaker is there to help end the chaos that exists in that present moment. They are problem solvers. It is one of the reasons we see them as blessed people.

To be a peacemaker means that you are able to identify the wrong in the world and have a hope to end it. The ending of that chaos may look like simply lending a helping hand, or it may be as complicated as confronting a bully. A peacemaker's role is in its name. A peacemaker makes peace in a world of chaos. God calls all of us to be peacemakers because, like peace in chaos, we bring light to a dark world.

Remind me to be a peacemaker. Teach me each day to recognize what that means and allow me to be the light in a dark world.

49

Each Day Has a Purpose

In the day of prosperity be joyful, but in the day of adversity,
consider: God has made the one as well as the other, so that
no one can discover anything that will come after him.

ECCLESIASTES 7:14

There are days that are good and days that are bad. It is a truth that all would find agreeable. There are days where we find victory and days that bring defeat. There are days filled with joy and days overcome with despair. One element that is often forgotten about the quality of these days is that each day comes with a lesson. Every single one of us can take a moment to learn from each and every day. God desires for each of us to gain wisdom from the lessons provided from each day. It is our response to these days that allow us to grow closer to Him, or grow farther away.

When we think about the best day we've ever had. Most of us can point to a day that was amazingly special. It may have had close friends or family present. It may have given rest that we so desperately needed. It may have provided an adventure that drove us to become better. When we remember the bad days, we almost have that same vivid memory. Some of us remember a day of hardship, a time when we were driven to work to the bone. Some of us remember a loss, a person that was dear to us that has left us. Some of us go back to a place of heartache, a place of tears over the brokenness felt in the day. Whatever the kind of day we have lived, there is always something important to say about the day. Each day gave us an opportunity to learn. God created each day with a purpose.

This brings us to a place where we must ask ourselves a few questions. How do we respond to the joy or devastation found in a day? What can be learned from these moments? What is God trying to teach me during this time? Whenever these moments arise, there is an opportunity that comes with them. Do we choose to learn, or do we choose to remain ignorant of the lesson being provided?

Learn appreciation in the times of rest. Learn thankfulness when around family. Discover bravery in the moments of adventure. Remember joy when there is the loss of a loved one. Master perseverance in the times of hardship. Find trust in the moments of heartache. God may not have provided the negativity of the day, but He always supplies a lesson. He always gives a chance for us to be able to learn something valuable in each and every moment. It is up to us, however, to recognize that moment of identifying the purpose.

Allow me to be able to recognize the purpose
in this world. Allow me to look at each day with
the ability to learn from every moment that You give.

50

God Always Gives More Joy

Many are saying, "Who can show us anything good?"
Let the light of your face shine on us, LORD.
You have put more joy in my heart than they
have when their grain and new wine abound.

PSALM 4:6-7

~

There was once a farmer who attended the same church as a teenage boy. The farmer had made it a bit of a tradition to hire four or five teenagers from the church to work on his farm each year. The boy worked alongside the farmer, tilling the field and preparing it for harvest. When harvest came, the boy stood proud looking out at all that he and his friends had accomplished. The farmer simply tilted his head in acknowledgment and walked back to his home to notify the market that he was pleased with the harvest. The boy, however, was frustrated with the farmer. At church, the farmer was a man of laughter, but on the farm, he seemed to be nothing but stoic. When he asked the farmer why he wasn't as happy with him like he is at church. The farmer simply grinned and said, "Boy, I'm more proud of what you do eternally than what you do in a field."

Most of us have encountered the good in the world. Most of us have been able to recognize when things are good. We seem to be in a season of satisfaction from time to time. We seem to have enough money or all of our bills seem to not be so daunting or our workload is manageable. Even if it only lasts for a few days, there is a great deal of joy that comes from the moments of abundance. Even in these moments, however, we can find ourselves still recognizing that something is missing. Everything is still all well and fine, but there is almost an instant recognition that there will come a time when this abundance has to end. It, like everything else in this world, leaves us inspecting the world to find out what is missing. What is missing, however, is not something of this earth, but it is of heaven.

Like the farmer, he knew he was pleased with the harvest, but he was fully aware he would eventually have to prepare the field again. He knew one good harvest would not be enough to sustain the joy in his soul. The farmer was more concerned with the joy of heaven. He knew that heaven would be more than enough to sustain him. He was fully aware that the joy provided by the harvest was temporary but the joy provided by God is something that would last for all eternity.

Look to God for your joy. The joy He provides will be given on a level that makes the world's joy look as it is: second best.

51

Don't Fear Suffering

*But even if you should suffer for righteousness, you are
blessed. Do not fear what they fear or be disturbed.*
1 PETER 3:14

⁓

We would all be liars if we acted like there wasn't any suffering in this world. We live in a world that is filled with hardship. It is what makes this life one that is so difficult. We see sickness, heartache, and persecution sprinkled throughout this world on a daily basis. If we allow it, the negativity of this world will be enough to make a black mark on our hearts. No matter what it is that we do, that is something that we cannot allow. We cannot allow ourselves to be engulfed in the fear of the world, nor can we be disturbed by it. The reason? It is because we are blessed.

Suffering is a part of life. It is something that all of us should probably know by now, but there is something important to say about this suffering. Many of us have probably seen suffering for selfish reasons. People who have taken advantage of others will inevitably suffer. A student that always copies homework will suffer the inevitability of being tested. A husband that is unfaithful will suffer from the truth coming into the forefront. A child that steals suffers the condemnation of having to return what was stolen. Whatever it is, we have definitely observed people that suffer for the wrong in their life. Suffering for the sake of righteousness, however, is something completely different.

Suffering is negative. I think that is something in which all of us can find agreement, but suffering for what is right has a weightlessness to the burden of suffering. It does not change the unpleasantness of that suffering, but we are still able to live with a sense of freedom in that time of suffering because we know we are living by what is right.

You know a brother or sister who is living in sin, and you try and hold them accountable like you would expect someone to do for you. However, when the sin is brought out into the light, the person rarely acts with a sense of gratitude and graciousness. They get angry. They become hurt. They may start calling out the sin in your life as a defense mechanism. They may even ostracize you from elements of their life. In short, they try and hurt you the way they have felt hurt by the light shining on the darkness.

It is because of all of this that so many are so terrified of the suffering that comes from being a light in the world, that they hide their light from others. They decide that the suffering is not worth it. The sad fact is that this could not be farther from the truth because it is the truth and light for which we are suffering.

Remind me, Lord, that suffering is worth the truth that I am putting out. Allow me to walk with grace and strength in this time of suffering, and allow me not to cower away from taking the righteous path.

52

Complete Joy

*"I have told you these things so that my joy
may be in you and your joy may be complete."*

A ll of us have joy. It is something that many of us experience on an almost daily basis. Joy can be found in the little things and in the big things. It can be found in the big moments like when we get a promotion at work, or our child makes good grades on their report card, or we are finally able to get a new car. Joy can also be felt in the small moments: like the first time our head hits the pillow, or we are able to make it to our jobs without heavy traffic, or we are able to come home and find that the chores have already been taken care of without being asked. Whatever it may be, there are hundreds upon thousands of things that bring us joy. The problem with these forms of joy, however, is that they are incomplete.

There is always something missing with all of the joy that the world brings. When we place our blessings and successes without realizing that these opportunities for joy are actually gifts, we rob ourselves of a greater joy. We are, essentially, settling for the joy that the world brings us when we could be having that joy expanded with the blessing of heaven. To put it simply, we are settling for a sugar cube when we could be having a brownie. We are saying that the appetizers are enough and that we don't need the main dish. We are saying that a picture of the vacation getaway will suffice when we could actually have the vacation. Simply put, we are settling.

God does not want us to settle. He does not want us to simply have the joy that comes from the world. He wants us to take these moments of joy with Him already a part of that joy. Whenever you get that promotion, do it with God. Whenever traffic light, don't look at it as plain luck; look at it as a gift from Him. Whenever your child performs well at school, it is not simply your child's hard work, but also a gift God has given to this child to set them up for success. Whenever the chores are finished and you are able to lay down, it is not simply a fluke that they were finished before you came home, you were loved by God so much that He blessed you with a family that cares for you so that you might find rest. Joy is something that almost all people can find, but the world can only give so much of it. In order to feel complete with the joyous moments in life, have God be a part of it, and recognize that this joy is a blessing from Him.

Thank You for the joy in my life. Thank you for being a part of my life so that this joy may be one that is complete. Remind me that the joy You give is one that makes me whole.

53

We Are His and He Is Ours

I am my love's and my love is mine; he feeds among the lilies.
Song of Songs 6:3

❧

One of the most amazing parts of Christianity is that it is described as a relationship. God is not simply a being that we worship. He definitely deserves that, but worship is not all that He wants. One of the most used concepts throughout the Bible is the fact that God wants to "know" us. He wants a relationship with us. He loves us.

It often reminds me of marriage. Whenever you stand before God with your future spouse, you make a promise. The promise may capture many different elements, but at the end of the day, it all comes down to the same concept, we promise to be theirs, and they promise to be ours. No matter all of the difficulties that may come with life, there is that promise that we will stand by this person, and they will stand by us. It is a simple promise, but there is a great deal of weight to that promise.

As strange as it may seem, God wants the same with us. God wants us to be with Him and He wants to be with us. God wants to stand by our side in times of difficulty and hardship, and He wants us to seek Him during those times. He wants to celebrate with us when we experience victory and triumph, and He wants us to give Him the glory for those moments of joy. God wants to be with us to comfort us in times of heartache and suffering, and He wants us to seek Him out during those dark times in our lives.

God wants us to love Him, and for us to be loved by Him. It is one of the simplest notions, but there is so much weight to the sentiment. God gave everything for us. God gave His Son for us. God has shown His love for us since the very beginning, and He continues to love us now. How can we not love when His love is so vast and so overwhelming? How can we not take on the love that has been poured out for us on a level that we will never be able to comprehend? God's love is one that has always been there for us and will always be present as well. His love is something that takes on a power that will never be fully understood by any of us. He has given us a love that wants to abide in us. Love, however, is only complete when both parties give that love to one another. God may love us with everything that He has, but we will never know how complete that love is unless we allow for that love to be in us and our love to be in Him.

Lord, Thank You for loving me. Thank You for making it so clear how much You love me, even if I may not be able to understand how much. Allow me to take that love in me, and place my love in You.

54

Love Even in the Difficult Moments

*A friend loves at all times, and a brother
is born for a difficult time.*
PROVERBS 17:17

⌒

A friend is one of the most valuable things we will ever know in this life. They are a source of laughter and joy and can often distract us from the negativity in our lives. Friends, however, change when that negativity cannot be avoided. The friends that are there for celebration only will often leave. They will often assume that continuing the friendship is not worth dealing with the negativity. Many of them will return after that dark season has passed, but some may not return out of fear of that difficult time coming back. Certain friends, however, make a great change. They become more than friends. They become brothers and sisters. They become family.

Many of us have been through these seasons. We have lost a job or lost a loved one, or we have a rebellious child or an unrelenting boss. We begin to struggle financially, or we have to deal with the frustrations of paying for something that puts us in a negative situation. Whatever the reason may be, all of us have had to deal with some time of darkness. Every single one of us has lived in a season of unknowing and despair. Difficult times come. It is a reality that many of us have had to come to terms with, but the light in these dark moments are often the people that surround us and love us during this time.

One woman's story about healing from a car accident is one that brings light to the kind of people that were in her life. The car accident was one that broke one of her legs severely. She would have rehab for two months after the cast finally was taken off. She would have to be driven there for the first month. In that month, her friend, Sarah, drove her every day that she had rehab. Sarah laughed with her and sat with her every step of the rehabilitation process. Her role in the healing process was nothing major, she only sat with her and talked with her as she always had. She did not pour a great deal of extra effort into their friendship, Sarah simply drove her to a building, sat in that building while her friend's rehabilitation took place, and then drove her home or they would go out to eat afterward. Sarah looked at this season as a time to be there for her friend. The woman, however, saw Sarah's actions as more. You see, Sarah had only acted as the friend she thought she should be, but the woman no longer saw Sarah as a friend. She saw her as a sister. The woman saw Sarah as family. How good is it that God provides friends that act like family?

Allow me to be a good friend. Allow me to love at all times, and act as a family member during the difficult times.

55

God - 1; Death - 0

Where, death, is your victory? Where, death, is your sting?
1 CORINTHIANS 15:55

~

Death is one of the scariest things that we have to deal with in our lives. People often point to a list of fears that they have to take on, but most of these fears can be avoided. If one is afraid of the dark, then turn on a light. If one is afraid of public speaking, then keep the speaking down to a conversational level. Death, however, is the only thing that cannot be avoided. So many people in this world view it as the end. They view it as the only thing that will ever be able to overtake us permanently. There is a sense of finality to it. This, however, cannot be further from the truth.

The reason why death is so terrifying is the fact that it is at the tip-top of the unknown. There are so many unknowns that get reasoned with over and over again, but the fact is that in death so many do not know what happens. For some, it is the end. There is nothing else. There is no consciousness or anything of the sort. For others, you just go into an eternal sleep, never able to wake up again. Both of these point to death's victory. Both of these point to the notion that there will come a time when death takes us over. This victory, however, is not in the possession of death. It is in the possession of Christ.

Because of Christ, we are able to live throughout eternity because of our faith in Him. Christ took on death. He took on our sin and died a painful death—making it seem that not even He could overcome the power of death.

He was laid to rest in a tomb. For three days, His body did not move, but it was on that third day, that He was raised. He burst forth from the clutches of death. He stood and went out of the grave—taking away any victory that death once had. It is because of His resurrection; it is because of His being brought back to life that we can all have peace and triumph over death.

It is still a concept that is almost unfathomable to us, but the beauty of this notion is that it does not matter. We do not have to understand the mystery as to how Christ triumphed over death, the same way we do not have to know how the sun rises. We can simply accept that it has happened. We can take joy in knowing that death no longer has a hold on us that have faith in Christ. Because of this, it does leave us asking the questions, "Where is your victory, Death? Where is that sting?"

> Lord, I am in awe of Your power. I am in awe of all that You
> have done for me. Thank You for overcoming the grave,
> and taking away that pain and fear of death we all once had.

56

Encouragement Is Necessary

Therefore encourage one another and build
each other up as you are already doing.
1 THESSALONIANS 5:11

~

A phenomenon that has taken over the athletic part of our culture is the notion of obstacle course races. They are filled with obstacles that test one's endurance, one's strength, and one's mental fortitude. Some of these are three miles long and others go all the way up to ten to fifteen miles long. They are physically draining and a grueling task for our body to undertake, and yet, people flock to the challenge. They pay hundreds of dollars to participate in these races throughout the year. From the outside looking in, it would seem that this would be the undertaking of crazy people, but some of us probably know someone that has participated in one of these races or maybe you have participated in one yourself.

One runner's description of the events, however, gives us a bit of understanding on why people jump into these races with joy and excitement. She said, "I love it. I hate getting dirty and am a bit of a neat freak, so it would seem like this whole thing isn't for me. There's mud everywhere. Everyone is sweaty, and you end up filthy by the end of all of it. So why do I do it? I do it for the friendships made there. You end up getting in a group of anywhere between five to ten people and we're all helping each other through it. All of us are cheering for each other and helping each other get over the obstacles.

Sometimes you know these people, but more often than not, you end up making new friendships that allow you to help and encourage each other through the race. That, to me, is the best part. It doesn't matter how you got there, we're all on the same team."

There is something very powerful about her words. She points out something that is so necessary to our development and care as people. Every single one of us, no matter how prideful we may be, need some form of encouragement from time to time. All of us desire to be a part of a team that wants everyone to succeed. It does not matter what the challenge is before us. What matters is the ability for us to be able to overcome that which is in our way. For many of us, we become timid and often shy away from all of the challenges in life. If we feel like we cannot accomplish something we often will not even try, but an encouraging word can make all the difference in the world.

So go out. Encourage others. It does not matter what it is. Even if it's something as simple as making copies at work, encourage those that work alongside you and allow yourself to be encouraged as well.

Allow me to be encouraged. Allow me to take the kind words that others give me and have them fuel my will. Remind me to encourage others. Remind me to show others love through encouragement.

57

Tears Show We Care

Those who sow in tears will reap with shouts of joy.
PSALM 126:5

～

All of us have shared a tear from time to time. Ask any mother, and she will probably say that she had spent many nights crying for her children. One boy, in particular, talks about his mother at his wedding reception. The bride had said her thanks to everyone there and spoken in depth about her bridesmaids and her parents. There were laughter and a few tears, but it was what one comes to expect from a bride the night before her wedding. The son, however, was a bit atypical. He looked at his groomsmen, said one or two words that implied inside jokes that kept that one table roaring with laughter. For his father, he thanked him for his wisdom and told his father he loved him with strong, yet tearful, eyes, but his mother was a different story.

For his mother, he apologized. He looked at her and gave a list of apologies that caused her tears throughout the years. Some were humorous, like apologizing for leaving open the refrigerator. Some were hard to hear, like sorry for accidentally losing a family heirloom. Some were heartfelt, like sorry for not being there when she needed him home. He continued to go through the list of little things, apologizing to his mother for all that he had done throughout his life. At the end of the speech, he told her he loved her, and he was thankful for all of those apologies that built up over the years because they were all lessons that would form him into the man he had become, and the husband he hoped to be.

The mother stood, and hugged her son tightly and took the mic and brought it to her face. With tears forming in her eyes, she looked at her son and said, "You stupid boy. I never cried because I was upset with you. I always cried because I loved you. I always cried because I knew that which God had blessed me with, would one day leave to bless others. It was heartbreaking every time I thought about my little boy leaving, but there was also joy because I knew one day you would find someone to bless in ways that you blessed me and in ways that I will never know. I raised you with tears in my eyes, and I will praise God for the man you have become with even more."

Many of us will never know the level of love some people will have for us. Some of us will never understand how some people can love us as much as they do. What we should know, however, is not that we make others cry because we've hurt them; sometimes tears are out of love and out of joy.

Lord thank You for the love in my life. Thank You for the tears,
for I know that they are simply markers of how much I care
for these people and how much joy I find in them.

58

There Is Nothing Better than Sharing a Meal

When Joseph saw Benjamin with them, he said to his
steward, "Take the men to my house. Slaughter an animal
and prepare it, for they will eat with me at noon."
GENESIS 43:16

~

It is one of the concepts that every single one of us has. No matter what the occasion, whenever we are united or reunited with anyone, there is almost this reflex of setting up a time to meet for a meal. It is also rarely ever something that just happens. Plans are normally made. Sections of time are blocked off to enjoy a meal together. These plans, however, are rarely ever made with anxiety. There is normally a joy to these plans.

For many people, they often think about Thanksgiving. There are many dishes and desserts planned for the family. We remember traditional recipes that were taught to us by our grandparents. We also acknowledge when other people try to come forward with their own "new" take on those recipes. They are never quite as good, but we allow it.

Why do we get so much joy out of these moments where we meet for meals or these moments where we prepare meals for others? It is fairly simple if we take the time to think about it. In regards to the meeting with others for meals, we have shown these people that we care about them. We have shown that we are both willing and excited to take parts out of our time to spend it with those we care about over a meal. With the holidays, we show something even more important. We show these people that in times of celebration, we reserve for them a place and prepare for them a meal because the holidays are meant for family, and we see them as such.

There is a joy that comes from sharing a meal with others in any context. It simply shows that we are willing to spend time with others. No matter what it is that we have together. It could be steak and potatoes, or hamburgers and hot-dogs. It can be sushi if that is what you enjoy, but whatever it is that you decide to eat does not matter. What matters is that there are people that love you enough to share that time with you. There are people that love you enough to prepare a meal for you.

God wants us to care for others. There are many ways to do this, but one of the most powerful ways to show that you care about someone is by preparing a meal for them. It shows that you spend time on the way you care. It shows that you give the effort to make sure that they are sustained. When preparing a meal for others, you're doing the work of God, for you are working to take care of their needs.

Lord thank You for those that have shared meals with me.
Thank You for those that have prepared meals for me. Allow me
to be able to take of others the way they have taken care of me.

59

His Peace Is Stronger than the World's

"Peace I leave with you. My peace I give to you.
I do not give to you as the world gives.
Don't let your heart be troubled or fearful."
JOHN 14:27

Peace is a temporary term in our world today. If we were to take a look throughout history, we might find that peace has always been celebrated, but only rarely has it ever been taken as permanent. Let us take America, for instance. In the 1700s, one could say that there was peace with England, but eventually, tension rose and we found ourselves in the Revolutionary War, or if we take a look at the World Wars, there was a brief period of peace between the two, but there was an ending to that peace as well. Even in our own country, we have seen moments of peace that were halted by the necessary change that threw us in a civil war, and if we were to take our country today, would we see a nation that seems peaceful? Of course not. We are so politically divided as a nation that people scream at each other depending on who you voted for.

The point is this: Worldly peace is a temporary one. No matter how hard we might try, many of us will never come close to gaining permanent peace on earth. There is not a treaty or law that will ever guarantee a permanent peace on this planet. That kind of everlasting peace can only come from Christ.

It is a special kind of peace that Christ has given us. He left us with this peace in knowing that one day He will return. No matter how bad the world may get or how frustrating our situations may become, Christ will return.

This peace is not a peace like the world gives to us. It is a peace with a promise that cannot be broken. The world has made promises to us many times. Handshakes are given. Smiles are shared. Armies are removed from other countries. Treaties are signed, and an overwhelming sense of hope is given to all of the nations. There are even institutions created to manage this peace. This peace, however, is a false peace. It is a peace that comes with an unknown expiration date. It is a peace that will end in one way or another.

Humanity has come to know the reality of the world's form of peace. We have all grown to naturally not fully trust the peace that is offered to us in this world. It is something that many people glue themselves to news stations trying to ascertain when the trouble will fall upon them.

This is not what God wants for us. Christ has left with us a peace in understanding that this world is far from perfect and that one day He will return. That is our peace. Even though the nations may be at each other's throats. We serve a mighty God whose Son will one day return and with Him bring peace.

Lord, I know the world is far from perfect. Allow me to let go of the worry I hold with world and instead, take the peace You have given us.

60

We Will Not Be Shaken

Cast your burden on the LORD, and he will sustain you;
he will never allow the righteous to be shaken.
PSALM 55:22

~

Do you ever feel like the world is trying to break you? Does it ever seem like the obstacles of each day cannot be overcome, or worse, that they are trying to overcome you? No matter where it is that you may find yourself, many of us can probably think of a time when the weight of the world seemed a little too heavy. Sometimes it seems like our burdens are too much for us to carry on our own. The truth is that sometimes you might just be right. Whether it is trying to care for family or make it home from work or even find time to rest, sometimes the burdens of this world are too heavy for us to get anything done. What do we do in these situations? Well, the Bible is pretty clear on this one. We are to give our burdens to God.

This seems like such a simple thing to do, and yet, we see so many of our Christian brothers and sisters that do their best to carry the weight of responsibility all on their own. Why is this? Well, when we get right down to it, people don't exactly like admitting that they need help. Most of us are not fans of the idea of letting anyone know that we need some form of assistance. Because of this, we've trained ourselves to not even allow God to know our burdens, which is silly because of the all-knowing nature of who He is. The fact is that all of us are to go to Him in prayer. God will take on our burdens and sustain us during this frustrating season.

There is a certain word, though, that is pointed out in this verse: *shaken.* God will not allow us to be shaken in our trials. The reason is that whenever we come to God in prayer to take away our burdens and to sustain us during these dark times, we end up finding that there is something powerful in God's response. Most of us have probably come to know that when we go to God in prayer, we find ourselves in a place of peace. We find ourselves with an understanding that whatever may come has been placed in God's hands. We know that whatever challenges and obstacles that may arise in the future, we have placed our burdens in God's hands. It is an incredibly powerful thing to be able to humble yourself before the Lord and admit that there is something we cannot handle on our own. When we place our burdens in the hands of God, how can we be shaken?

Thank You for listening, Father. Thank You for allowing me to be able to come to You in times of need. Take my burdens, Lord, and allow me to not be shaken in the hard times of life.

61

Love Covers Sin

Above all, maintain constant love for one another,
since love covers a multitude of sins.
1 PETER 4:8

~

One of the most amazing things that we have is the concept of love. Growing up, we often heard different forms of affection such as *like*, *like-like*, and *love*. Whenever we heard children coming home talking about one of these levels of affection, we quickly learned that there was a hierarchy to this love.

Most of us have heard of high school sweethearts, but only a few of us have seen couples that have been together since elementary school. After ten years of marriage, Suzanne discusses her relationship with her husband as one that evolved from like to like-like to love. She discussed this with her eight-year-old daughter who came home stating that she liked a boy at school and asking her mother how she knew her father was the one to marry.

The woman looked at her daughter and said, "I first liked your father on the playground during our first day of fifth grade. He was new to the school system and didn't know anyone. I found him particularly peculiar because he was sitting in the grass, picking dandelions, and blowing them into the wind. I asked if I could sit with him and we blew dandelions together for most of our recess. He became a friend and started joining me and my group of friends for parties and church events. When we were teenagers, I admitted that I had developed a crush on him, and he reached down behind me and plucked a dandelion and asked me to be his girlfriend. After a few months of dating, I had moved from 'like-liking' your father to loving him. He admitted he had loved me for quite some time as well." It was then the daughter asked, "How did you know you loved him?" The woman grinned, "Much like that dandelion, your father could be a weed sometimes. He made mistakes. There were times he acted selfishly; there were times when he would drive me absolutely up a wall, but it never made me stop loving him. I could always look past those imperfections and love him in spite of them, just as he has loved me in spite of me and my selfishness."

When the girl asked, "Is that what made you marry him?" She looked at her daughter and said, "That's what true love is. It is a choice that allows you to look past the bad and choose the good. You love them as they are not as you want them to be. It's a lot how God loves us. He loves us even though we are so imperfect."

It was after that the girl looked at her mother's wedding picture and understood. She saw her two younger smiling parents holding each other while her mother's bouquet was held in the air showing the most beautiful flowers and in the midst of them, a single, solitary dandelion.

Lord, thank You for loving me. Thank You for loving me even though I don't deserve it. Thank You for giving a love that covers my sins.

62

It Is So Good to Be Loved

Because of the Lord's faithful love we
do not perish, for his mercies never end.
LAMENTATIONS 3:22

O ne of the most wonderful things in the world is the fact that there is a love that is faithful. What does it mean to be faithful? What are the implications of such a word? The implications of the faithful are that they will never fail. It means that no matter what may happen, whatever is faithful will always endure. No matter what obstacles may come, whatever is faithful will be able to overcome. This is a concept that is difficult for us to understand. It is because there are so few things in this world that could be considered faithful. Some might even argue that nothing on this planet could be considered faithful. People lie. Job opportunities fall through. Marriages end. This world constantly gives us reasons to not have faith. God, however, is very different. It is His love that is faithful. It is His love that has proven time and again that it and His mercies will never end.

Faith is something that is often tested. It is a notion that we are put in difficult situations time and again. The things of this world test our faith on a regular basis. People that we have had faith in have given us reasons not to place our faith in them. Careers that we thought we would always be able to work somehow ask us to leave. Spouses that have promised to stand by us till death are now trying to leave. There can be so much heartache that can come from putting our faith into the aspects of this world.

Our God, however, is an amazing God. He has proven His love from the beginning of time. From the beginning, He created us. He made a plan for us. He freed us. He sent His Son for us. His Son died for our sins. His Son is preparing a place for us, and we have faith that His Son will one day return. It is easy for us to have a faith in the love of God whenever it has shown to be true time and again over the course of history. It is because of His love that we can have faith in knowing that we will not perish. We will not be brought down to condemnation. It is because of His love that we are shown mercy, time and again, for the sin in our lives. God has given us a love that is easy for us to place our faith. God has given us a love that will last forever, and we can always place our faith in the things that have proven to stand the test of time.

Lord, thank You for loving me. Thank You for giving me a love that I can place my faith. Remind me each day of the mercy You show me, and give me the ability to know Your love is everlasting and never-failing.

63

The Greatest of the Great

Now these three remain: faith, hope, and love—
but the greatest of these is love.
1 CORINTHIANS 13:13

~

When we take into account all that we are called to have, there are many great things that we should aspire to gain. Faith, hope, and love are simply by-products of an authentic relationship with Christ. All of these are incredible for incredibly different reasons.

Faith gives a sense of knowing and understanding that whatever God's will is, it will have. It allows us to live in the present with a knowledge that whatever may come will be endured because God endures. Faith, simply put, is an assurance of the good that God will give.

Hope allows for us to be able to have our eyes on the future with joy. There is no worry with hope. When our hope is coupled with our faith. We can live in the present—enjoying the blessings that God has given us each and every day. We can also look to the future; not with anxiety or fear but with a joy and excitement in knowing that God's will shall be done.

Both of these are tremendous. They are some of the most amazing parts of our following of Christ, but no matter how great these may be, they are silver medals when compared to the golden love. We can have faith like the greatest of holy men, but if we do not love then this faith is hollow. We can have the hope of the greatest optimist but if we do not love, then this hope is, sadly, pointless. All three are incredibly important, but love is the one that must exist in our lives. Yes, God wants us to have faith in all that He does and continues to do in our lives. We are called to have faith in God. Yes, God wants us to have our eyes on the future with a sense of hope, not a sense of anxiety, but God has given us a love beyond all understanding. Without us having love, then what is the point of faith. How can you have faith in something you do not love? Without our love, hope is simply a gamble and guesswork. Isn't our hope a little more assured when we have a foundation of love?

Love, as many of us have come to know, is the most wonderful thing we could ever have. It is the foundation of our faith. It is the refuge for our hope. It is what brings the meaning to what would be meaningless without it. Whether we want to admit it or not, love is so necessary to our hope and our faith. Without it, we are simply a people that have a hope and faith with no purpose, for it is God's love for us and our love for Him that provides the purpose to the hope and faith that He provides.

Father, remind me to love. Hope and faith will some days
come more naturally to me, but I know that these are nothing
without love. Allow me to constantly be reminded of the love
You give me, and allow me to have that love in all that I do.

64

His Peace Is Perfect

*You will keep the mind that is dependent on you
in perfect peace, for it is trusting in you.*
ISAIAH 26:3

~

I t seems that people are trying to find the perfect peace of mind every day. We plan vacations. We set aside time. We maybe even have a special room that some of us mark as our quiet place. We go out of our way in every single way that we can conjure up a sense of peace. The problem with this is the problem with most things in this world. It is not perfect. No matter how good the peace may feel, it is never good enough to be lasting. We can find an escape that gets our minds as far away from the chaos as we can, and yet, we will still find ourselves in a troubling situation. That problem is that no matter how far we go, no matter how long we stay, no matter how much money we put into it, we will eventually have to return to the chaos of our daily lives. No matter the peace we seek, it is not perfect because it simply does not last.

Because this peace is a temporary one, we inevitably find ourselves in a place of frustration every time we find some form of relaxation. Every single one of us knows this feeling. You've put weeks into planning the vacation. The day has come. You're off to your getaway. Then, after a few days, you realize something. You think about all the emails that are going to have to be answered. You wonder just how much work has piled up on your desk since you've left, or maybe you even start to look at the computer you've brought with you. You think that maybe working a little here will make work a little bit easier when you finally return.

It may be something as simple as the weekend. You've been thinking about Friday night since Tuesday morning. You think about the quiet that awaits you. You'll sleep in or maybe go on a day trip, and then one of the most difficult times of the weekend shows itself: Sunday night. You're frantic. You start having anxiety over the week that is coming before you, and you've proven, once again, what all of this is about. It's about the fact that you've lost the peace that you were so looking forward to having. It is not your fault necessarily. It is simply because the peace you have sought out is one that is not everlasting.

God knows this, of course. The world will never be able to give something that is eternal. We have a need to reach out to God for that everlasting peace. There is a peace in knowing that whatever trial you may find yourself, God has given the ability to overcome this time. His peace is not like the world. It is a perfect peace.

Remind me to be able to look at the frustrations of my daily life and call on You for peace to help me through them. Allow me to be able to reach out to You more and more. Give me peace, Lord. Amen

65

There Is a Reason We Respect Authority

Remind them to submit to rulers and
authorities, to obey, to be ready for every good work,
to slander no one, to avoid fighting, and to be kind,
always showing gentleness to all people.

TITUS 3:1-2

~

There is a reason why we follow the law. Even though speed limits may not be in the Bible, they are still one of many laws that are to be followed. God wants us to follow these rules, but He also wants us to do more than just that. There is a call to have a gentle spirit with other people. No matter how frustrating we may get from time to time, we are still called to reach out to others and to love them. We are still called to be able to treat people with respect and dignity.

It, honestly, reminds me of an older gentleman in the town where I was raised. Many of us probably know a similar old man if we think back to our younger years. His name was Nick. He was always seen serving his community in any way that he could. He volunteered at the fire department and helped mop floors once a week. He worked in blood drives. He organized town festivals. He put extra coupons on the windows of police cars. He was a man that served in any way, shape, or form. He would never speak ill of any of them, nor would he allow himself to become flustered by those that did not respect the authorities he served throughout the week. Instead, he would only encourage those to come with him and see why he did all that he did.

He finally found someone to come with him one day, just to see why he did what he did. It was a young man that finally agreed to his challenge. Throughout the day, he saw firemen walk with anxiety over the potential of calls. He saw police officers filling out mountains of paperwork. He heard hospital workers talking about how they were understaffed and in need of supplies. He even was able to learn that the mayor sees a counselor because managing the town's budget was such an enormous undertaking. He learned the reason why we submit to authority.

It is often difficult for us to even think about the notion of submission to authority. Some of us like to challenge our parents, let alone the government, but we find that there is a reason for this submission. They do not rule over us. They serve us. Our communities are filled with people that have authority over different things, and we can gladly submit to them, not because they are in charge of us, but rather because they serve us. How can we not be happy to serve those that are in the service of serving?

Lord, allow me to recognize that those with authority are also those with responsibility. Allow me to acknowledge that my submission is not a giving up, but rather a respect.

66

Faithful Over the Little Things

"His master said to him, 'Well done, good and faithful servant! You were faithful over a few things; I will put you in charge of many things. Share your master's joy!"
MATTHEW 25:21

~

Most of us have been here before. The boss walks in and places a major responsibility on your desk. It may not even be that major of a responsibility, but it is definitely the biggest one you have ever been given. It might seem daunting. Maybe it's a report over something that will take a few months to accomplish, and you only have two. Maybe it's a project that will require oversight that demands you staying after work hours once a week. Maybe it's even getting a "Yes" from someone that normally gives a "No." Whatever the responsibility, there is this desire to do well for those that have authority over us. Maybe we respect them. Maybe they have a promotion available that we want. Maybe it is even the difference between having a job and not. Even if we do not like the person that is over us, we respect the fact that they are and naturally wish to perform well for them. We want to show our dependability by completing the tasks that we are given.

God is no different. When we think about our faithfulness to Christ, it is really such a small thing to be faithful over. He is the proclaimed Son of God. He walked on water. He turned water into wine. He calmed the storms. He healed the sick. He made the blind see. He made the handicapped walk. He brought life to death and defeated death by being raised to life. Jesus has given us so many reasons to have faith in who He is. He has proven through His time in ministry and through His sacrifice that He is someone very much worth following. Our faithfulness to Christ is such a little responsibility when we think about it. It may definitely be a difficult task for us to be able to follow after Him each and every day, but the decision to do so should be an easy one. He has proven that He is one that is worthy of our following. He has proven that He loves us on a level that none of us will ever understand. He is more than the most respectable boss could ever be. He is the perfect Lamb. He was the perfect sacrifice for our sins. Whether or not He is worthy of our faithfulness is not the difficulty, but it is, rather, the standing up, picking up our cross, and following. What is our reward for this faithfulness? Well, it's heaven. It is the place where joy is unmatched by anything in this world. How can we not be faithful when that is our reward for such faithfulness?

Remind me to be faithful. Allow me to take time each day
to follow after You and Your example so that I may bring You joy.

67

The Answer to What Is Unseen

Now faith is the reality of what is hoped for,
the proof of what is not seen.
HEBREWS 11:1

As a child, many of us can probably remember the family vacation. There was always a discussion on where and when it would be. As children, however, it was always a difficulty for some of us to have this conversation because there was almost this skepticism over whether or not it would happen. Some of our family members would mention it almost every other day, if not every day. They would look forward to the day of its arrival with hopeful eyes, while others of us would look on with disbelief on whether or not it would really happen, but then, as the big day became closer, there were little hints that would pop up with a promise that it was, indeed, coming. You would see suitcases be taken out of closets. People would start writing up itineraries. Others would start making lists of what needs to be done before the departure. There now seemed to be signs that what was promised now seemed to be on the horizon. It was now within our view. We started to make the move from skeptic to believer. We became hopeful over the future. We looked forward with optimism. In a sense, we started to have faith.

Many of us probably remember a time that we felt the same about God. Some of us may even still be in this season. What is the reason for this? Why is it so difficult for us to believe what is promised? For many of us, we refuse to acknowledge the early signs. We do not take the time to listen to those that have a faith greater than our own. We do not look forward with eyes that are hopeful about the future. Simply put, we put our trust in what we can see over that which has been promised to us. As Christians, we are called to do so much more than that. It requires us to be able to look forward and have joy over what is to come, even if it means that we may not readily be able to see it at this time.

Of course, that is how faith works, isn't it? We are called to do more than trust what we can see from our perspective. If that were the case, faith would not even exist. Faith is the joy and assurance over what is to come. It does not, by any means, promise that we will be able to see and understand all that is promised to us. That is the challenge and joy of faith. Like a child preparing for vacation, we have faith in the great adventure that lies before us. Even if we do not see all that is on the path, we have faith when we travel that path with Christ.

> Lord, give me faith. Allow me to be able to look forward
> to the future with a sense of joy. Allow me to trust in
> what I can't see and know that someday I will.

68

We Can Rest in Him

I lie down and sleep; I wake again
because the LORD sustains me.
PSALM 3:5

~

Many of us have probably heard this famous prayer for children. It is a rhyme that eases a child's soul while preparing their eyes to close as a slow cadence brings a child to a place where they feel secure enough to sleep.

Now I lay me down to sleep,
I pray the Lord my soul to keep.
May God guard me through the night,
And wake me with the morning light.

Some of us probably remember this rhyme when we said it with our children as we prepared them for bed. Some of us may even remember a time when our parents said it with us before we went to sleep. It is something that has provided young children with something that has helped them sleep for years and years: security. For children, and even for some adults, the time before bed is an apprehensive time. The lights are turned off, and we are enveloped in something that our hearts and minds know should be avoided: darkness. It is no wonder many children fear the dark. Why should they not? It is one of the biggest things that we are all constantly told to avoid, and yet, we surround ourselves with it in our most vulnerable state. Darkness, whether we want to admit it or not, is something in which all of us are at least uncomfortable. When watching a scary movie or walking in a basement, what is the first thing we try to do? We try and find the light. Children that are afraid of the dark, however, are told something that many of us have to tell ourselves, "There's nothing to be afraid of."

There is such a truth to this for reasons that few of us will ever admit. No matter how little we can see in the dark, all of us trust that there is nothing to be afraid of in the dark because we are protected by the Light of the world. With that prayer above, we acknowledge that it is with God that we trust our souls and we pray that no matter what lies in the darkness, God will protect us through the night so that we might wake the next day. It seems to be something that has worked so far. So take on the trust of a child. Allow yourself to close your eyes. Give the protection of your soul to God and allow Him to protect you through the night so that you may wake again at the first light of morning. We serve a God that protects us in the moments where we cannot protect ourselves, and there is a promise that our souls can never be plucked from the protection of His mighty hand.

Lord, thank You for protecting me. Remind me every day that even though I may be in a season of darkness, I can still find rest in You. Allow me to believe this and rest in knowing that You are my protection, my light in darkness.

69

The Sweetness of a Friend

Oil and incense bring joy to the heart,
and the sweetness of a friend is better than self-counsel.
Proverbs 27:9

~

There are many things that can bring a joy to our hearts. Many material things can often bring temporary happiness to our lives. Even things that are by-products of some materials can bring back memories that supply a joy that is more than superficial. For instance, the smell of a certain baked good can bring you back to a place and time where the family was a focal point to our lives, or a certain kind of touch can often bring us back to a place and time where joy was a natural feeling to all the good that resided during that time. This joy is by no means a bad thing. There is nothing wrong with having things that bring back a sentiment of true joy, especially if those things can trigger certain memories that had a foundation set in love. All of these are opportunities that we can perform ourselves, but none of these can even hold a candle to the joy of the moment with the people of these memories. It is like settling for the scent of a meal instead of actually having it for consumption.

This is where those special people come into play. Many of us can probably think back to a time when we were able to be with these people, and what is the first thing that we do? We plan a reunion with these people. It may be something as simple as planning a meal or going on a vacation with them or even taking the time to pick up the phone and simply talk to them. There is so much more worth to a friendship than simply the reminiscences of one. Friendship and family are things that deserve to be lived out, not just remembered. They are things that we are called to enjoy because of the sweetness of these moments.

There is a joy to this even when there is a loss. We hold onto the joy of these people that have gone to be with the Father because of the fact that there is that promise for a reunion. Even when we have lost them on this earth, we know that there will one day be a time when we can all be in heaven together and hold each other again. We will acknowledge that this reunion is because of the victory of Christ over death.

What do we do with this knowledge? It is simple. Instead of looking back on all of the moments you may have had with this person, reach out and make new memories. Even though we have the promise of reunification with these people, even after death, we all still feel the guilt and remorse of not taking advantage of the time we have with them right now. So go out. Make new memories with the ones you love. There is a sweetness to it that you'll never be able to fully explain.

Lord, thank You for friends. Allow me to pick up the phone and reach out to these people. Allow me to be able to make new memories with these people and appreciate the sweetness of my time with them.

70

Hope in What You Can't Yet See

Now in this hope we were saved, yet hope that is seen is not hope, because who hopes for what he sees? But if we hope for what we do not see, we eagerly wait for it with patience.

ROMANS 8:24-25

If you ask any camper that has experience in survivalism, they will often tell you that one of the biggest things that can ever happen is getting lost in the woods. It can be one of the most terrifying things to happen to a person. Being lost in the wilderness is something that many hope to never have to happen to them. There are many different ways to be rescued from this questionable time, but one of the ways that is most efficient is by simply sitting still and making the area you are in a safe one.

It is something that many campers are told whenever they go out into the woods. When one couple was asked how they made it out, they made a simple statement. The wife said, "We had hope. We took the time to get the tent out of our pack and set camp. We cleared the surrounding area, built a large fire, and waited. We had made the mistake of not charging our radios and had left our compass and map in the truck before we set out. It was a mistake that we don't plan on ever making again. There was a loose rock while we were hiking, and my husband slipped and broke his ankle. We had packed enough food to where we could probably make it a few days if we needed to, but I gathered food just in case as my husband did his best to start a fire.

After the fire was started, I continued to get enough wood to last us through the night and started marking trees to lead me back to him as I explored the area for a water source." She continued on like this as she discussed different ways she and her husband worked to survive out in the wilderness until help could arrive. When asked how she didn't lose her cool, she said this, "I kept my mind busy. I knew that if I didn't, the circumstances would start to get to me, but something that my husband and I have always read about these situations is that if you simply do the right things then you can have hope that the right things will happen. We made camp. Built a big fire. Told people where we were going and to expect a call from us after a day. When that call didn't come and a day had passed, it was only a few hours later that our smoke was spotted and we were found. We didn't have to see what was coming to have hope in it."

God is the same way—there are so many things that we take hope in because they have been promised to us. We can know that by doing what is right according to Him and His statutes, we can have hope in the future.

Allow me to do what is right by You, Lord. Allow me to chase after You in such a way where I can have hope in what I cannot yet see.

71

The Golden Rule Is a Desire for Respect

*"Just as you want others to do for you,
do the same for them."*
LUKE 6:31

~

We all have heard of this rule. Most of us were made aware of it at an early age. It is something most of us were taught by our parents, but even if not by them, it was taught in church or during our early years in kindergarten. Whenever it may have been, many of us became aware of this rule at a very young age. Why were we taught this first? Why, above all of the things that could have been taught, do we choose to teach our children the importance of treating others the way in which they would wish to be treated? The answer is a simple one. It is one of the first stages of one of the most desirable characteristics in life: respect.

So many of us, whether we decide to admit it or not, care deeply about the notion of respect. Many of us would like to liked by everyone. That is a common human characteristic, but almost all of us have a need and desire to be respected. Whether we are at work, or school, or even at church, there is this nearly innate desire for us to be respected by our peers. Why is this? Why do we have this strong desire toward being respected? Well, the answer to that is also a simple one. It goes down to a deeper level. Respect is one of the first building blocks toward something that we are all called to have for one another: love.

Think about the Golden Rule for a moment. As we would want people to do for us, that is what we should be willing to do for them. That shows a great deal of respect, but it also shows the first steps of love. It shows that you love someone enough to think about how you would want to be treated, and then you go out of your way to treat them that way.

When we carry out the Golden Rule, we show so much more than a simple level of respect. We show that there is such a love we have for someone that we are willing to consider the ways in which we love to be treated and do our best to carry out that love for others.

It is more than a simple lesson for a child. It is something that still holds weight for us today. Go out into your community. Show the people in your life that you respect them, of course, but also go further. Show your love by thinking about how you would wish to be treated and treat them as such; there is such a joy from carrying out this Golden Rule. When you know that it is love you show when you carry it out, you'll realize that it is love they show when they carry it out with you.

Lord, remind me each day to show my love for others by treating them the way I would want to be treated. Allow me to show respect for others, but also carry out love for them as well.

72

Our Hope in Him Brings Strength and Courage

Be strong, and let your heart be courageous,
all you who put your hope in the LORD.
PSALM 31:24

⌒

Many of us have a favorite outfit. There is something about that certain shirt or the certain shoes that just give us a sense of confidence. We almost feel like we can take on the day because of the fact that we are now walking with a sense of courageousness that is normally not found without that part of our outfit. Inevitably, however, that courageousness and strength seem to fall apart when something unfortunate happens; like the shirt rips or the shoes become too worn down to wear. It's enough to ruin our day. This, however, is one of those things that is absolutely asinine when we stop and think about it. You haven't gotten where you are because of your fashion choices. It has probably taken months and months of hard work, if not years, but alas, it never fails. Whenever we place our hopes in the things of the world, we inevitably find ourselves in a place of despair because of the fact that these things are not everlasting.

Even thinking about things that have always seemed to be there will one day let us down. It is because of this that we cannot put our faith and hope in the things of the world. We cannot place our hope in the things that are temporary. We must place our faith in that which is eternal, and that is our Lord.

God, unlike that shirt or those shoes, is someone that has always been. He has existed since before the beginning and He will continue to exist after the end. He is outside of time. He does not wear down with time, nor is He able to be overcome by any constant beating down that may exist. Whether we take the time to realize it or not, God always is and always will be. He is the source of ultimate strength and courage that will carry us through the end of our days in this life. He has never been overcome. He has never been defeated. He is the overwhelming source of victory. It is because of this reality that we can draw our courage and our strength from Him. We can come to Him in weakness and from Him, we can draw strength.

God has not called us to be a people that are controlled by weakness. We are called to rely on him as our source of strength. We are called to go to Him so that we might be seen as servants of a mighty and powerful God. There is no need for us to place our hopes in the world, for it can only give that which is temporary. Instead, fall before the Lord, and He will give you strength and courage.

Lord, I come to You in weakness. I recognize that I am weak,
but with You, I can stand and stake on the day that is
before me. Allow me to be strong and courageous with You.

73

God Gives a Great Spirit

For God has not given us a spirit of fear,
but one of power, love, and sound judgment.
2 Timothy 1:7

~

We can always take heart in recognizing people that have chased after God. They are always fairly easy to point out. It is not by any measurement of their outward appearance. It is so much more than what the outside could ever show. Instead, these people are recognized by their spirit.

There was an older woman named Nelda at a small country church that had one of these recognizable spirits. She was celebrating her 90th birthday and the crowd was all pointing to how spry she seemed to be for someone that was approaching a century of a life spent on this earth. It was something that seemed to baffle the congregation as they celebrated with the elderly woman. When the pastor spoke on her, he was quick to point to the verse above in describing her. He said that he had never known a woman that had a more powerful, loving, and wise spirit.

She was always seen leading the charge on new opportunities for the church to serve the community. She showed her power each time for being one of the first to volunteer for any event the church would host or participate. She was never afraid of time constraints that would hinder her performance. Though her body had become weak over the years, she would always say that you don't need your legs to show your love.

That sentiment was what helped people to see the level of love she had for people. It did not matter who you were or who you belonged to, she was never afraid to greet people with open arms. She was always willing to shower people with love every single time she came into contact with them. Whether you were a visitor of the church or a regular attendee, you never left the building without having a minute to talk with Nelda. She would not allow you to leave without a hug or a gift or a verse that she had felt the Lord place on her heart.

Her willingness to share was her mark of wisdom. She was always very knowledgeable about the Word of God. Some even speculated that she had the book memorized. It was because of this deep, reverent relationship that she had with the Bible that she was able to share a great deal of wisdom that she had acquired over her lifetime. People would often come to her because they knew that they could trust her counsel on certain subjects, especially in regards to the matters of the church. Even the pastor would seek her out from time to time when needing counsel on how to better minister to his congregation.

Nelda was a woman that was known for her age, of course, but it wasn't the number that shocked them. It was the fact that many knew she was not long for this world, and yet, Nelda would continue to stand and share her powerful spirit with those around her. There was no fear of death; Nelda had a spirit that was too young to be afraid of something as silly as death.

Lord, allow me to let go of my fearfulness and take on a spirit of power, love, and wisdom. Remind me each day that You have given me a spirit that is too powerful to be encumbered by fear.

74

Set Your Minds on God

Set your minds on things above, not on earthly things.
COLOSSIANS 3:2

⟋‿⟍

There is a charge to this verse. Some could probably argue that could even be seen as a command. There is a point to this. There is a reason why it is so direct. It is because of the fact that there is so much wisdom found in this statement. There is a certain word, however, that points to something so much more than what we care to realize. The word is *set*. What is the significance of this word? Why does such a small word hold such a significant weight? Whether we would like to admit it or not, there is a powerful sentiment behind the idea of "setting" anything.

When we think about the word *set*, we bring ourselves to a place of recognition. When we set anything down, it is because we trust the foundation on which the item has been set upon. Whenever we set ourselves before a race, it is because we have come to trust that which will propel us into a sprint. Whenever we allow something to set in construction, it means that we wait for something to become a foundation that is trustworthy. To set anything is to acknowledge that it is something that can be trusted. That is why we are told to set our things on what is above and not on what is on the earth.

Think about the things that are exclusively on earth. We have people, places, governments, even places of nature. All of these, however, are able to fail us. No matter how trustworthy they may seem, they are all things that are capable of failing us. With people, they have the downfall of sin that keeps them from being completely trusted with being our foundation. People lie, cheat, and steal. All of us are guilty of those to some degree or another. With places, no matter how economically successful they may be, or how properly they may be maintained, every town can go back to a time when they had been failed by their area either by natural disaster or by improper governance. With governments, every few years a group of people will inevitably feel like the world is going to end because whoever takes up an office will fail in one form or another. Even with the world itself, with all of its natural beauty, no matter how strong each may seem, all of us can remember moments when the winds blew and the earth quaked to the point at which these natural wonders were nowhere near as permanent as they may have seen.

The reason why we say to set our minds on the things above is because the things above have long proved and promised to be everlasting. God will never fail and will never be overcome. He provides a foundation that can be trusted, and it is upon His foundation that we should find ourselves set.

Lord, allow me to keep my eyes on You. Allow me to set myself on the foundation that You provide. Remind me daily that this world cannot be trusted wholly, for it is You that is everlasting.

75

He Will Never Leave Us in the Face of Danger

"Be strong and courageous; don't be terrified or afraid of them. For the LORD your God is the one who will go with you; he will not leave you or abandon you."

DEUTERONOMY 31:6

~

Strength and courage is something that we've discussed a great deal in this book. There is a reason for it. It is because there can be no joy—there can be no happiness—if our hearts are consumed by fear. A great deal of fear stems from the feeling of being alone. It is more difficult for us to be consumed by fear if we are not alone. It is one of the many reasons we often try not to go anywhere we don't know well by ourselves. We do our best to be able to take on challenges with others. If we do not do so, fear and apprehension is almost a necessary quality that will grow from the situation. This is not how we are to behave, however. We are called to be stronger than this. We are called to be able to take command of these questionable moments with a strong spirit. How are we able to do this? How are we able to take on an attitude of success? Well, it is rather simple. Whether we want to admit it or not, the moments that success seems like a likely possibility are almost guaranteed when we feel like we are not alone.

This is the same way with God. There are so many different obstacles in this world that can make us feel as if they are insurmountable, and yet, we find ourselves capable when we acknowledge that no matter how difficult the obstacle may seem, we are never alone. God is with us.

If we take the time to think about it, we can all probably remember a time when someone said that they would be with us, and yet, it fell through. It is one of the things that creates difficulties in our ability to trust anyone, even God. Many of us have worked on a project or have put our minds to the test with a partner or a team and found ourselves alone in the process. We all probably remember that one partner in school that no one wanted to work with simply because it was a guarantee that you would be left to do the work on your own. This, however, is not the case with God.

God will not leave us. He will not forsake us. We do not have to be afraid of what lies before us because of the fact that we can act courageously in knowing that God is not going to leave us alone. We will not be left to deal with the task on our own because He loves us.

Lord, thank You for not leaving me during the difficult times.
Remind me that You are always with me. Remind me that
I am not alone. Allow me to take on what lies before me, and
allow me to do it courageously, knowing that You are with me.

76

Your Roots Matter

"The man who trusts in the Lord, whose confidence indeed
is the Lord, is blessed. He will be like a tree planted by water:
it sends its roots out toward a stream, it doesn't fear when
heat comes, and its foliage remains green. It will not worry in
a year of drought or cease producing fruit."
JEREMIAH 17:7–8

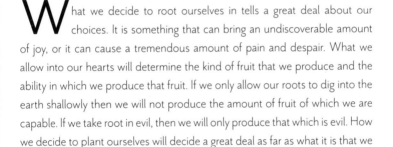

What we decide to root ourselves in tells a great deal about our choices. It is something that can bring an undiscoverable amount of joy, or it can cause a tremendous amount of pain and despair. What we allow into our hearts will determine the kind of fruit that we produce and the ability in which we produce that fruit. If we only allow our roots to dig into the earth shallowly then we will not produce the amount of fruit of which we are capable. If we take root in evil, then we will only produce that which is evil. How we decide to plant ourselves will decide a great deal as far as what it is that we produce. Where we place our trust is also where we will find our roots. We can only grow from the things that have our trust.

When we think about our lives, there are many things that can come from what we trust. If we place our trust in our jobs, we will probably produce a salary and a level of status and recognition, but we will never be able to produce a sense of satisfaction if our roots are constantly digging into a place that gives a culture of climbing a ladder. If we place our trust in good times, then we will produce a fruit that desires to have fun. We will find fruit that is sweet but rots our souls because we assume relationships are only worth keeping if they are seen as producing a good time. The point is this, whatever it is that holds our trust also will determine the quality of fruit that we produce. The two examples mentioned, however, produce a fruit that is unable to be sustained. When a difficult season arises, those roots will find themselves shriveled because their source is one that is superficial. Where, then, should we place our roots? In what should we place our trust?

The answer is one that many of us have come to know well. We are called to place our trust, our roots, in God. When we are rooted in Christ, we produce a fruit that brings a joy that is sustaining to yourself and others. When the times are difficult, planting ourselves in Christ is an option that only becomes wiser because God's love is like a stream. It constantly flows—giving life and sustenance to those He touches.

Lord, remind me daily of where my roots are. Allow me to produce a fruit that is sustaining to myself and others. I know that it is only through planting myself deeper in You that I am able to come closer to You and produce a fruit that is pleasing to You.

77

Love Because He Loves

Dear friends, if God loved us in this way,
we also must love one another.
1 JOHN 4:11

⌒

L et's be honest. There are some people that are easy to love and others that are not so easy. There are some individuals that come into our lives that seem to only bring joy with them, and there are others that are responsible for a great deal of the joy that's been taken away from us. Whether we would like to admit this or not, there are people we easily like, and people that sap our energy from trying to like them.

Many of us operate similarly to the way we did in school. Even though we've grown a great deal and have gained the ability to be able to show respect for each other, it is another thing entirely for us to be able to love all of these people. Maybe there is a coworker that drives you mad. Maybe you deal with a boss that is difficult to work for. Maybe the in-laws are just about all that you can handle. Whatever the case may be, many of us have certain individuals that can find a way to live just under the surface of our skin. This, however, is not the Christian way. This is not what we were called to do. How do we remedy this behavior? Well, the answer is quite an easy one. We need to be willing to alter our perspective. We cannot think of these individuals from our own perspective, but rather from the view of Christ.

What exactly does this mean? It means thinking about what Christ has done for you. Despite all your shortcomings, all your flaws, all of the uncharacteristically nasty things that you've done, Christ still loved you. He still loved you enough to give His life for you. He still loved you enough to die for your sins so that you may live with Him forever in heaven. He still loves you so much that He is in heaven, now, preparing a place for you. When we take this into account, we desperately need to come to a conclusion. We need to be able to recognize that Christ loves these people that frustrate you so much with the same level of love that He has for you. God is not expecting you to be able to die on a cross for the sins of these people. That love has already been shown, but the point of it all is this. If Christ were able to love you enough to die for your sins and their sins, then why is it a difficulty for you to show them love because Christ has shown you love? How good is it to know that God loves someone just as much as He loves you? How can we not love them when we know that? How can we not take joy in that?

Lord, thank You for loving me and remind me to love others like You loved me. Allow me to be able to show love for those that are difficult to love. Remind me that they are loved by You just as much as I am.

78

Carry Burdens and Have Burdens Carried

Carry one another's burdens;
in this way you will fulfill the law of Christ.
GALATIANS 6:2

~

There was once a woman who had two twin boys. She taught this lesson with chores. Though the boys were twins, they had very different interests, even when it came down to chores. The way chores were taken care of in the house was through randomly drawing chores at the beginning of the week and those chores would be placed on the refrigerator with the responsibility attached to the name. It was a method that she would come to use until the boys left for college.

The chores would mainly consist of yard work, such as weed-eating, hedge-clipping, lawn mowing, and raking. Those were the main four outside of the typical cleaning of rooms and trash being taken out. The boys may have looked the same, but they could not have been more different. One was more precise and the other was better at shutting off his brain to do manual labor. The reason why this is brought up is because of the fact that it never mattered the chores that they were given. The precise one would always take weed-eating and hedge clipping and the one that could turn off his mind would do the monotony of lawn mowing and raking. The boys would always look at the refrigerator and give each other a wink—knowing who would inevitably do which job.

The boys went off to college together. They both roomed together as well. In their dorm, they held the same rhythm. One would clean with tasks that required precision and the other would do the more time-consuming but easier tasks. When the mother came to visit, she smiled knowing how the boys worked to keep the place clean.

Years later, the boys asked their mother if she ever knew they traded jobs on an almost weekly basis. She responded with a smile and said, "Boys, I'm your mother. I knew you switched, and I always knew you would." When they asked why she even bothered putting the list on the refrigerator, she looked up to them again and said, "I knew one of you liked the ways of some jobs and the other preferred the ways of the other jobs. I wanted to see if you boys loved each other enough to carry the weight of the others' burdens, or would you simply carry the weight of your own without trying to share the burden with the other. You both made me proud; both of you chose to trade. Was it easier for you? Yes, but it was always a way to show that you were willing to take the weight off of each others' shoulders."

God wants us to operate the same way. We are not called to simply live a life where we push through on our own. We are called to share our burdens with one another. We are called to take on the burdens of others as they have taken on ours.

Lord, thank You for those in my life that have taken on
my burdens. Allow me to take on the burdens of those that
need my help. Remind me of the importance of helping others.

79

It's a Funny Thing

Our mouths were filled with laughter then, and our
tongues with shouts of joy. Then they said among the
nations, "The LORD has done great things for them."
PSALM 126:2

Two farmers were standing out behind their barn of a Christmas tree farm. They were brothers-in-law. Both had married the farmer's only two daughters. The farmer, because of his age, entrusted his land to the young men. The regrettable thing about this trust was that both men had no farming experience. One was a science teacher and the other drove a truck. The father, however, said, "I have faith ya'll will be just fine . . . just give it time, and don't be afraid to ask for advice." The young men spent the next five years doing just that.

Now, Christmas tree farming is an interesting field. Most crops are ready to harvest within a year, but Christmas trees can often take a minimum of four years before they are ready to be harvested. Because of this, the father had a small staff that worked on the farm. There is still a great deal of work that goes into the maintenance of the trees. A farmer will take a seedling, tie it gently against a bamboo stick, place the stick into a hole, and close the hole. The stick ensures that the tree will grow straight. After the tree is grown, however, it must be trimmed in order to ensure that it grows in the shape of the traditional Christmas tree. Farmers will take machetes and swing them at an angle thousands of times throughout a day to ensure that the tree grows the way that it should. The two brothers did this for four years before they could see the fruit of their labor.

When the young men were standing behind their barn, they looked out to a field that had once been empty now filled with trees as far as the eye could see. The two looked at each other and laughed, for a teacher and a truck driver had accomplished a great thing. Their faith allowed them to push forward while knowing little, and through that faith, they produced greatness.

It is one of the most amazing things that we can ever experience—that God will do great things through us despite whether or not we know how to do what needs to be done. It is laughable when we take the time to think about it. God works through us on a level that allows us to be able to take on what we have never done. He allows us to have moments of success even in times of confusion. When we see that success—that greatness after it is all said and done—we cannot help but laugh, for God has decided to use us to accomplish amazing, wonderful things, whether we know how to do them or not.

Thank You for using me. Thank You for allowing me to
be able to take on many things even though I may not know
how to do them. Give me faith, Lord, so I may look back at Your
wonders and laugh at the way You used me to accomplish them.

80

We See What Others Can't

So we do not focus on what is seen, but on what is unseen.
For what is seen is temporary, but what is unseen is eternal.
2 CORINTHIANS 4:18

Most of us, if not all of us, have been put in a position where we've had to defend our faith. As frustrating as it may seem, the most difficult part of being a Christian is sometimes having to defend our faith to skeptics. We shouldn't be shocked by this. Instead, we should probably acknowledge that it will probably happen to all of us, and this is a good thing. How can we take joy in a faith that has never been tested? How can we grow closer to God if we have never had to explain why we believe what we believe?

One young woman discusses her time in doing this. She was sixteen. She was in her science class, and she found herself defending the faith from a skeptical teacher. His question for her was, "How can you believe in something that cannot be seen or measured?" Her response was a simple one at first. She said, "Do you believe in the magnetic fields?" The teacher was quick to say, "Those can be measured. That is the problem with you Christians. You point to the invisible and think because it can't be seen, then it is in the same ballpark as God." She took a moment. She looked down quietly and as the teacher turned to get back to work, she asked him, "Sir, are you happy?" The teacher questioned her response for a moment and then said, "Of course, I'm a very happy man." She said, "How do you know?" He responded with "I just do, and the brain gives off chemicals that give me happiness." This is when she grinned, "Can you measure those?" The teacher, frustrated, looked down and said, "No, each brain is different and there is no way to measure the amount of that chemical needed to produce happiness." He knew what was coming next. He knew there was going to be the smugness of a teenager waiting to talk him down, but all she said was, "Well, I believe that some things exist that cannot be seen or measured too. I guess we're not that different."

God cannot be seen or measured, and yet, so many people all over the world find a way to believe in Him. Even though He has never been able to be viewed on a scientific level, Christians are able to keep their eyes on Him with absolute assurance. They are able to look past all of the frustrations of the world and follow after the unseeable. There is a reason for this. Faith is more than a simple hope; it is a knowing. Christians are able to recognize the great work that Christ has done in their lives. For them, it does not matter whether or not the world can physically see God, for the Christian sees His fingerprints left on their hearts.

Lord, allow me to keep my eyes on You. Allow me to recognize all of the good that You have done. Sharpen my faith, and remind me to keep my eyes on You even when others can't.

81

Honest Love

Love must be without hypocrisy.
Detest evil; cling to what is good.
ROMANS 12:9

⌒

There was an older woman at a church that had a sentiment that had become famous within their congregation. The members seemed to like it so much that they started to adapt it to their lives. She would often say, "The Lord says I have to love everyone. It doesn't mean that I have to like everyone." This sentiment was something that would become an issue within the church. People started ignoring each other. Cliques started to form. Members of Sunday school classes were starting to feel alienated. The congregation had become a hotbed for divisiveness. Then, it finally happened. During a meeting, a churchgoer finally stood and said that they had become an outsider in a church they had been raised. When people stood to defend their behavior, that same older woman watched, in horror, as a quote that she had coined was now used to defend the actions of dissension within the church.

How many of us have seen this? How many of us have seen people use the Bible to explain why they treat some people differently than others? Regardless of how we may feel about people, our love for them cannot be hypocritical. We are called to show everyone the same level of love God has shown for us. Obviously, we cannot sacrifice our lives for every single person with whom we come into contact, but we are called to at least have the same loving relationship for them that Christ had for us. No matter the wrong that has been caused or the disrespect that has been given, we are called to still love and care for everyone we come into contact with. We cannot simply write people out of our lives because they don't necessarily treat us the way that we think we deserve to be treated. When we start ignoring people because of hurt and shame, it is only a matter of time before our unconditional love starts coming with conditions. That is something that makes our love hypocritical. God did not call us to love everyone. When we show them that we don't like them, it doesn't matter whether or not we "love" them. That love is something that will destroy hearts. It is a love that will bruise souls. It is a love that is hypocritical. After hearing her words twisted, the woman stood and apologized for teaching hypocrisy.

God has given us, time and again, the model for love that we should follow. Our love should show friendship. Our love should show respect. Our love should show joy. It should bring a peace to others, and it should move past the imperfections that we see the same way God's love moved past our imperfections. The love we should have for one another is one that shows that we care for others. It should be a love that is shown, not one that is simply said.

Forgive me for the times that I have not shown love
to the ones who have hurt me. Remind me that all people
deserve to be loved. Make my love true and not hypocritical.

82

Joy in Mourning

"Those who mourn are blessed, for they will be comforted."
MATTHEW 5:4

⌒

Something that will always stand out about certain funerals is the fact that every now and again, we will come across a funeral where the mourning seems to be something that is overcome with laughter. It is something where a few of us will have our eyebrows raised. At one woman's funeral, the sons and daughters spoke on their mother's life. Their eyes were puffy. Bags had formed under their eyes. One could definitely tell that their nights had been long, leading up to that day. What happened, however, was so different from the expectations of the crowd. They started to tell stories that brought laughter.

One son spoke on one of his experiences with his mother, how she was a terrible cook in general but could always make some of the best desserts you could ever desire. He went into detail of her cooking, how she once figured out how to burn spaghetti, how she made a meatloaf that was tougher to chew than some steaks, or even how she wasn't paying attention and put hot pepper jelly with his peanut butter. The entire church was cackling with his stories, but he would always go back to her desserts. He would always point to her ability to make some of the best desserts. Tears started to form again. His voice started to crack, "I won't miss those meals, but God is lucky to have some of her desserts."

When the daughter came up, she talked about sewing with her mother. She discussed how she would hate sewing with her mother because of how talented her mother was compared to her at the craft. People would laugh again as she told stories of how her mother would, outright, tell her that her sewing was terrible, how her mother would often just laugh at how shirts she had sewn together had arms that were longer than the other. Then, tears began to come again when she said, "My mom's favorite sweater was one that I made for her. She would wear it all the time—hugging everyone with open arms to show that the left arm was three inches shorter than the right."

There was a mixture between laughter and crying with the people at the service. This was a blessing in itself. People recognized the sadness that was found in losing someone so precious, but there was so much joy that she had left behind. People definitely had mourned, but the laughter was the clear victor in the season of sadness. They were blessed and comforted in knowing that one day, they would sew together; that one day they would have her dessert again.

God wants us to hold onto the joy of the loved ones that go home before us. He wants us to acknowledge that within that sadness is a joy and peace beyond all understanding.

Lord, thank You for my time with my loved ones.
Allow me to appreciate the ones who are still with us and
spend time with them, but also allow me to take time and look
back with joy and peace with the ones that have been lost.

83

Remain in God and Remain in Love

*And we have come to know and to believe the love
that God has for us. God is love, and the one who remains
in love remains in God, and God remains in him.*

1 JOHN 4:16

~

O ver a lifetime, many of us have come to know the love that God has for us. We have probably come to realize that God loves us on a level that no one has ever been able to love us. It is because of this love that we have been able to realize that because God's love surpasses any level of love that we could hope to have, God must be love in itself. There is something incredible in that sentiment; that God loves us so much that His very identity is love. How can we not love God when this is the case? How can we not remain in this love?

Many of us have heard terms like this: "You are what you eat," or "You will become that which you seek." This does not mean that if one eats a bunch of cheeseburgers that they will become an actual cheeseburger, nor does it mean if one is constantly focused on their work that they will inevitably become the CEO of the company. It does mean that we will be identified by that which we pursue. If we pursue unhealthy foods, we will look like someone that only eats unhealthy foods. If we are people that only pursue our work, then we will be identified as workaholics. There is nothing on this planet that we can pursue with such tenacity that will bring us to a place where we actually become these things. God, however, is so different for amazing reasons. God's number one goal is to love. God has done so many things in all of our lives that would show that He is not just a loving God, but He, in fact, is love itself. He has shown us a level of love that no person on this planet could ever attain. He created us in His image. He opened the gates of heaven so that we might be with Him, and He gave us His only Son so that we would be seen as blameless in His sight.

God has pursued love on such a level that love is His identity. There is no greater love than His, and if we abide in His love then we abide in Him, and if we are abiding in Him, then His love is abiding in us. It is a love that is so wonderful and complex that we will never come close to understanding it. How can we not take joy over a love like that?

Thank You for loving me. Remind me to continue to abide in Your love, and remind me that this love is one that abides in me as well.

84

Give Mercy because He Was Merciful to You

"Be merciful, just as your Father also is merciful."
LUKE 6:36

⌒

We all mess up. It's a given. It doesn't matter how perfect we try to be, there will always be a time when we drop the ball. It is an inevitability. There will come a time when we make a mistake. One of the moments that can make all the difference in the world is the notion of mercy. Even though we can recognize some of the moments where we've had mercy given to us, it is one of the greatest difficulties for some of us to give mercy to others. As much as we hate to say it, we love to be forgiven, but hate forgiving others, and why shouldn't we? People that have hurt us don't deserve forgiveness. If they did, they wouldn't have hurt us in the first place, and yet, we are still called to forgive. Why is this? Well, it is because we have been forgiven. Whether we choose to acknowledge it or not, we are far from perfect, and it is these imperfections that have been forgiven by God. He has shown mercy on us. That is how mercy works, after all; it is forgiveness given to those that do not deserve it.

Many of us have had horrible things happen to us. We have been betrayed; we have had our hearts broken—leaving marks on our spirits that can't be forgotten. What is harder for us to acknowledge is that even those these terrible, unforgivable things have been done to us, it is very likely that our own actions have had the same effect on others. Many of us may point out that we've never cheated on a spouse, or stolen from someone, or committed a felony. Many of us may even point to all the good that we've done in the world to prove what morally upright people we are. This, however, does not prove anything. We all have sinned. We all have fallen short. Regardless of whether or not we want to admit it or not, we have imperfections that leave us with a need for mercy. Our imperfections have placed us where forgiveness is a necessity, and the beauty of all of this is that mercy has been given through the power of Jesus Christ on the cross.

God has shown us mercy for our consistent wrongdoing. He has given us forgiveness for the sin in our lives, and He expects us to have the same forgiveness for others in our lives. People are going to mess up. That is a given, but the wonderful part of all of this is that we serve a God that has modeled for us a merciful behavior to share with others, and in that mercy, we find a joy and happiness that is unparalleled.

Remind me to show mercy to others. Allow me to be able to realize that I have been forgiven and that I should forgive others as well.

85

He Guards Us

But the Lord is faithful; He will strengthen
and guard you from the evil one.
2 THESSALONIANS 3:3

~

I f one were to go to Buckingham Palace, one would inevitably see the fabled Queen's Guard. The men stand rigidly in the infamous red uniforms for two hours at a time multiple times a day for twenty-four to forty-eight-hour shifts. Millions of people have come from miles and miles to see Buckingham Palace. Their reasons are not traditionally to admire the architecture or even to maybe catch a glimpse of the Queen. Instead, millions and millions line up try and have pictures taken with the Queen's Guard. Though they have become somewhat of a novelty, the Royal Guard is filled with men that have been trained to be some of the highest quality of soldiers. They go through nearly six months of training before they are even approved for active duty. Though no one has attempted an attack on the Crown for quite some time, the Queen would have little to worry about in regards to an attack. Many of the men in the Royal Guard are rumored to be as well trained as some of the upper levels of the American military.

It is a tremendous feeling to know that we are secure. Many of us spend thousands of dollars a year maintaining an expensive security system. Some of us have dogs that would attack an intruder. Some of us take self-defense courses and martial arts training. Some of us sleep with a weapon nearby. Whatever you choose, there is something ingrained in our psyche that makes us want to seek some form of security. We all have some part of us that desires to know that whatever may come, we will be protected.

All of us go out of our way to seek protection, but there is a certain level of protection with which no amount of worldly training can even compare. There is a certain threat to which no earthly form of protection will ever come close. Evil is something that is a constant threat in our daily lives. Satan attacks us with confusion, temptation, frustration, and despair. These are attacks that slide past our exterior and strike at our cores. There is only one defense against these attacks. It is only through God that we can feel secure. He guards us from the depravity of the devil every single day. He keeps us from falling at the hands of a most terrible foe. With God, however, that foe is nothing. God has the power to keep us secure. He has the power to protect us from evil. It is because of His never-ending love for us that we find ourselves in a place of security and peace. It is in His protection that our souls can find rest and joy.

Thank You for protecting me. Remind me to not
lean on my own ways. Allow me to run to You for
protection for all the evils that are thrown at me daily.

86

Tough Love

Better an open reprimand than concealed love.
The wounds of a friend are trustworthy,
but the kisses of an enemy are excessive.
Proverbs 27:5-6

~

Have you ever had a hard talk with a friend, or worse has a friend ever had a hard talk with you? We all know what's being discussed. We see a friend that is not living life the way they should, or we may be caught in a season of sin ourselves, and then, it happen: the hard talk. It's never a pleasant talk. In fact, it is often these talks that put friendships to the test. Some friendships have even ended over the entrance of a hard talk.

There was once a young man that had to deal with a hard talk from his future wife. He was not taking the Bible seriously. He was not focussed on the Scriptures, and prayer was definitely not a priority in his life. Because of this, he would fall to temptation every now and again by staying up late with friends and skipping church the next morning. After a few months of this behavior and earnest attempts to try and motivate her significant other to take his faith seriously, she had had enough. She called him and asked the most terrifying question men could ever hear: "Can we talk?"

The young man, terrified, ran to his future wife and asked what was wrong. The girl, with tear-filled eyes, told him that she could not marry a man that refused to lead her spiritually. She called off their engagement until he proved that he could be more. The young man was hurt; he felt that he had not done anything wrong, and for a week, he allowed the break-up to finalize in his mind. His heart, however, had other plans.

After that week, he called her to tell her that he had realized something. He realized that he was angry with her, at first, mainly because he was unwilling to hear the truth. He said that his "friends" would say that he was better off without her, but even though it felt good to hear people support him, he knew something wasn't right. He realized that even though she was right, he did not want her to be right. This was not because of pride in admitting that she was right, but more so admitting that he was wrong.

There are so many times in our lives that people point out the wrong in our lives, and our reaction is inappropriate. Like the young man, many of us will initially become upset with the ones that truly love us, and push them out of our lives. We will seek out the people that will claim that we are right just because they think it will be what we want to hear.

God does not want this for us. God places special people in our lives that love us enough to point out the wrong in our lives. Does it hurt? Yes, but so does surgery. It doesn't change whether or not it's good. Embrace those tough talks, for they have been given from people that God provided to love you, And to answer your question. The couple did get married and are about to celebrate forty years of marriage.

Thank You for the tough talks. Thank You for giving people that love me enough to tell me the truth even when it isn't fun. Thank You for giving me people that love me enough to do that.

87

He Is in Our Corner

"The LORD will fight for you, and you must be quiet."
EXODUS 14:14

⌒

One of the most amazing things that I've ever seen was a boy's older sister standing up for her younger brother. The younger brother was barely five years old and found himself at the mercy of an eight-year-old bully. The older sister, twelve, had told the bus driver about what was happening, and the driver scolded the bully. The bully stopped his actions on the bus and then continued his tirade on the younger brother after the bus dropped the boys off at the neighborhood. After a few days of this, the older sister decided that action needed to be taken. As the bully started picking on her younger brother, the sister stood in front of her younger brother. After the bully saw that the older sister was willing to protect her younger brother, the bully laughed and said, "You're getting a girl to fight for you?" The young boy, still flustered, didn't say anything. At this moment, the girl pulled out her mother's perfume and began to spray the bully down. When he questioned why she did this, she simply responded, "At least my brother doesn't smell like a girl." The bully never bothered the two again.

There is something so good about knowing that there is someone in your corner. Sometimes it will make all the difference in the world. There are many people who feel so alone that they feel no matter what they do, they are not able to overcome the obstacles of life on their own, or worse, they feel too weak and exhausted to even try to overcome the problems of the world. Simply put, there are some battles that we cannot fight on our own. No matter how strong we are or how much preparation has gone into our work, there are moments where we need someone to do the fighting for us.

God wants to fight for you. He has fought for us on a level that we will never understand already. He fought the pain of giving up His Son so that we may live. His Son overcame death so that we could have everlasting life. God has already proven that He will fight for us in ways that we cannot comprehend. He wants to do the same now. He wants to be there for us. He is in our corner. Troubles will come that will challenge and sharpen us, but God will never allow us to be overcome. He will always stand and fight for us because of who He is. He is a God of love and protection. He is a mighty God that will stand for those that cannot stand themselves. In that we have joy and thankfulness.

> Thank You for fighting for me. Remind me every day
> that You are in my corner. Allow me to know that
> You will not allow me to be overcome.

88

Nothing Is in Our Way

What then are we to say about these things?
If God is for us, who is against us?
Romans 8:31

❧

I n Imperial Beach, California, there is the U.S. Open Sand Castle Competition. It is one of the largest events of the year. People come from miles and miles to be able to see all of the creations that sand sculptors carve and mold out of the sand. Sculptors will tell you that the largest challenges in creating the perfect sand castle revolve around the notion of timing and location. The sand sculpture has to be close enough to the ocean for the sand to be wet enough to mold into the creation desired, and the sculptor has to start at the perfect time to ensure that they have enough time to complete the sculpture. These sculptures become more and more elaborate as time goes on, but they all have the same thing in common. Regardless of whether a sculptor is an expert or a novice, their sculptures are all adherent to the ocean. No matter how large they make the sculptures, they all will crumble when faced with the incoming tide. This does not upset the sculptors. One has even said, "We could spend all day building a sand wall, and it would crumble . . . nothin' stops the ocean."

God operates so similarly to the ocean. There is nothing that can stop it. No amount of work done by man would ever be enough to keep the ocean from coming in for high tide. No one questions it, or tries to stop it; they accept it as a reality. There is an acceptance to truth. Even if we may not like it, there is always an acceptance to certain truths. We all get older. We all get slower. We all get tired. We all need rest. The sky will always be blue. Winter will mostly be cold, and summer will mainly be hot. There are some truths that we gladly accept. Laughter may not be the best, but it is good medicine. Listening will get you farther than speaking, and nothing can stand against God.

It is one of the reasons why this verse holds so much weight. It is a truth that all of us have come to know. Regardless of what the world may claim, God is the ruler over all. He has been found victorious in a battle that hasn't even happened yet. He cannot be overcome by anything of this world, even death. It is why this question is not sincere. It is a rhetorical one, for we already know the righteous power that God has. It is why the question in the verse above is already answered. If God is for us, who is against us? The answer is simple: no one.

Lord, thank You for all of Your power in our lives. Thank You for showing that there is nothing that can overcome You. Remind me daily that if You are for me, then nothing can stand against me.

89

Lift Your Eyes to Him

But you, LORD, are a shield around me, my glory,
and the One who lifts up my head.
PSALM 3:3

~

There are some days that just feel like a battle. We wake up and we already know that the day before us is going to be one that is going to sap a great deal of our energy away from us. Some of us take the time early in the morning to pray. We pray for God to help us get through the day. We pray that our actions may glorify Him, and then we go out into our day. We then do what we have come to do best. We work.

Every once in a while, we come upon a day when that prayer was needed on a level that we didn't expect. The workload is more than we anticipated. The day is longer than we thought. It is in these moments that we've become thankful for our prayer time with God.

We've acknowledged Him as our shield. We know that whatever may come will be something that we can handle. Whatever arrows may be fired at us throughout the day, we have been shielded from them so that we may endure through the day. We know that we can press onward for His glory.

We've prayed that we may glorify Him. We wear His banner so that we may be able to work for Him. In all that we do, no matter how much praise we may get, we know to point any glory we may receive to Him. God has given us the ability to be a mighty warrior for Him. No matter what may happen or what obstacle may come, we know that it is God that has given us the strength and glory to push through the toughness of the day.

In our battle through the day, however, something happens. Our heads are lifted. We take a moment to breathe. We look up for a moment and have a brief moment of rest. Why is this? Why have our eyes been drawn upward? The answer is simple. This looking up is to remind us why we are able to work through the obstacles that are before us. We are reminded that it is because of God's love that we are able to be shielded, that we are able to work for His glory. Taking a moment to look up and thank God for all that He has done is something that we so often forget to do. We say our prayer for God's protection and dive right into the battle and normally don't come out until the battle is over. In doing this, we are in danger of forgetting that God is with us. We get so caught up in the rhythm of the battle that we forget to look up and find that He is with us. When the day is long and difficult, look up, and find a joy in knowing that You are not alone in this time.

Thank You for being with me. Remind me to look to You in the times of frustration. Allow me to be able to look up from the daily battle and realize that You are fighting with me.

90

The Like-Minded Family

Now finally, all of you should be like-minded
and sympathetic, should love believers,
and be compassionate and humble.
1 PETER 3:8

~

Many of us go to church every Sunday for many different reasons. It might have a great kids program, or the pastor knows how to give a good sermon, or something about that potluck is just the pick-me-up we need once a month. Maybe the people at the church are friendly, or maybe they have a missions team that we love to be a part of. Whatever the reason may be, many of us have one thing that we all love about our church. We, for the most part, are all like-minded. We all, for the most part, feel similarly about what God is doing in the lives of the people in the church, and the church itself.

We all have the same joy when someone is baptized. We all nod when the pastor has locked into the meaning of Scripture. We all have joy when we hear a person has accepted Christ. We may have different backgrounds. We may have different political views, or outlooks on the world, but there is a joy in knowing that we all feel the same about the work that God is doing.

There is a reason why people use terms like "church family." It is because of the fact that we operate so much like a family. Sure, we may have arguments, disagreements, or altercations, but it is how we respond to those that make us a family. When we've hurt someone, we are to respond with sympathy. When we see that someone is in need, there should be a response of compassion, and whenever a member of the church comes to us to make us aware of a shortcoming in our lives, we are to respond with humility. Above all, though, we should try to find a common ground.

Luckily for us, that common ground is Christ. No matter the kind of conversation we have to have, we both should celebrate in joy that we both have been redeemed of the sin in our lives. We both should respond in thankfulness that we get to serve a mighty God. We both should come to one another with a spirit of like-mindedness. It is in those moments of like-mindedness that we are able to have real conversation. It is when we are both standing on common ground that we can righteously have open and honest communication. When we both acknowledge that we all have imperfections and that all of those imperfections have been forgiven, it is then that we are able to have joy with one another.

No one in a family is exactly the same. It is only a matter of time before we have a disagreement, but when we are able to come together and celebrate that we are the same, that we are all loved by an amazing, all-powerful God, it is then that we can celebrate our time as family.

Lord, thank You for like-minded believers. Remind me that we are all to be like-minded. When times happen that test my relationships with others, allow me to remember that they are family and should be treated as such.

91

He Is Our Refuge

The LORD is good, a stronghold in a day of distress;
he cares for those who take refuge in him.
NAHUM 1:7

~

There is nothing more distressing than an incoming storm. One man's pride and joy was his storm shelter. It was built just off of the house and was just about the size of the first floor of his home. It was furnished, had an emergency generator in case the power went out, and had enough food to last them three days if they had to stay down there. He called it his own "personal bunker." He bragged about it to his neighbors and would even give tours of the place to show them all of the amenities. He eventually even had cable installed so that he and his buddies could move their game nights to "the bunker." His wife finally agreed that it served a positive purpose.

Storms would come and go, and he would always insist on the family going to the bunker because he "wanted to get his money's worth," but it was one day that a major storm was beginning to brew. The weather stations were saying that there would be multiple tornados and strong winds throughout the night. It was so bad that schools were already prepared to close for the next day. The man prepared for the worst by going to the store to get food and supplies that would allow he and his family to make it through the storm and its aftermath for as long as possible.

When he returned, he found his friends and his neighbors parked outside of his home. Before he could question anything, the storm broke and he rushed everyone inside. It turned out that the storm was not as strong as they would have predicted. There was slight wind damage; some power had been knocked out, and there was debris on the road, but there was nothing too major to what had happened.

Weeks later, the man finally asked his friends at a game night why they came to him. One man's response was, "How could we not? Your place provided the most protection. Even when we were getting ready in my basement, all we could think about is how much safer we would have felt at your bunker. How could we not come?"

God shares many qualities with that bunker. In a time of distress, people flocked to a place that provided the most safety. We naturally seek out a place that will give us a sense of peace in a time of distress. For us, we've come to know that God is that refuge, that God is the offerer of that peace in the storm. No matter how dark the storms in our lives may feel, we can take joy in knowing that God is a refuge that will never be overcome.

Lord, thank You for being my place of safety. Thank You for allowing me to run to You when the times are dark.

92

Friends That Become Family

A man with many friends may be harmed, but there is a
friend who stays closer than a brother.
Proverbs 18:24

~

Jennifer's favorite time of year was something she had dubbed "Friendsgiving." It was a special time of year when she and her college roommate would make a Thanksgiving meal together and watch movies. They all happened to live so far away from home that it did not make feasible sense to go home on Thanksgiving. It was a tradition that the girls would come to look forward to every year. When the girls all graduated, it seemed like the tradition would end.

Months had passed. The roommates had kept in touch over the phone with short but pleasant conversations. As the fall season made its approach and families prepared for Halloween, Jennifer began to feel a sense of dismay. She assumed that her favorite time of year was just a season that had passed. She had thought about organizing it just like last time, but she did not want to be seen as a friend that was living in the past. The month of October passed, and quick conversations with her roommates came and went. She felt alone.

As Thanksgiving approached, she felt a slow happiness rise in her because she was going to be able for the first time to connect with her family. She looked for recipes and made plans to travel for the holiday. The weekend before, however, something happened. As she sat on her couch, watching a movie, she heard footsteps approach her home with hushed snickering. She stood to her feet, happy tears already starting to form in her eyes, as she heard three sets of knuckles knock on the door.

She opened the door to find her roommates—holding food and waiting to be let in to continue their tradition.

Friendsgiving still goes on today. The girls have now grown. They have all married and have had children of their own, but they all still make time for the weekend before Thanksgiving to come together for Friendsgiving weekend.

Sometimes, *friend* is not enough. The word simply doesn't cover what some people are to us. There are some people that surpass the meaning of friend and move into the territory of family. Some of us have come to know friends that are now viewed as family. We've come to know that there are people in our lives who God intended for us to have as a brother or sister. This is a blessing. It is a blessing to know that God has given us people who are so special to us that they have become family in our eyes. They may not share our blood, but they hold a bond with us that is just as strong as that of a sibling. Thank God for these people and continue treating them like the family they are.

Lord, thank You for putting these special people in my life. Remind me constantly of the goodness these people bring to my life.

93

Good Always Wins

Do not be conquered by evil, but conquer evil with good.
ROMANS 12:21

Something that is often discussed in many English classes is the concept of the "Hero's Journey." It is a fascinating concept that many teachers have used in order to illustrate the path that every hero will walk before the end of the story. There may be variations in the story, which is what makes the story original, but there is always that notion of a path that the main character must follow in order to reach his or her destination.

The first step is the innocence. The character is shown as being unassuming. They are regularly shown being your normal, everyday, person. They might have a few quirks or talents that make them special, but all in all, they are simply average. The next step is the call to adventure, it brings the character to a problem that must be solved. Whatever the issue is, they will inevitably be moved to the second step. That next step is the refusal of the call, for whatever reason, they do not want to take on whatever obstacle has been placed before them. There is a preparation time, but then eventually there is a return to the problem and the inevitable defeat of that problem.

So many of us go through a hero's journey of our own. There are times when the frustrations of life are so much that it feels like we will be overcome, but the fact is that we were not called to be destroyed. We were called to conquer. We were called to defeat evil with good.

Some of us may feel that there is so much evil, so much darkness in the world that we go into that step where we don't want to even pick up our sword to fight. This is a problem because our reasoning for not standing and fighting is a silly one. Why would we not stand up and fight evil when we know that we have the ultimate good on our side? Why would we simply sit idly by and allow darkness to consume our lives when we can put an end to it with the power of God? So many of us go in and out of each day with a spirit of defeat. This is a trick. This is a lie. Don't you know we have already won? All we are doing now is simply defeating the last remnants of a war that has already been won. We are dealing with an enemy that has already been defeated. So don't allow the evil in the world make you think it has a foothold. Don't allow the darkness in this world overcome the light that God has given you. Stand, and take joy in knowing that this enemy has already lost. The battle is already won.

Lord, thank You for being with me in the times of battle.
Allow me to stand and fight each day knowing that You
are the source of the good that will conquer evil.

94

Harmony Appreciated

*How good and pleasant it is when
brothers live together in harmony!*
PSALM 133:1

~

Alison was the mother of two teenage boys. Those two boys could not be more different from each other. One was an athlete. The other was in the arts. Because of their differences, it was often that they were at each other's throats. Fights would start at dinner over who would have the last roll. Arguments would start at the bathroom door over how long one of them was taking. Snide remarks were said just loud enough for one to hear as they walked by each other's rooms. Alison was worried that her boys would never get along. She was worried that her boys would only grow to hate each other. When the boys were old enough, they each went their separate ways. One brother stayed close to home, and the other moved across the state. Alison's heart was broken. She thought that her now-adult children were locked in their disdain for one another.

Something, however, changed when her youngest son came by the house after work. He walked up to the door, phone against his face, and laughing. When his mother let him in, he got off the phone, hugged her, and began telling her about his day. Before he got too deep into his story, the mother stopped him and asked who he was talking to on the phone. He grinned and said that he was talking to his brother. This was something that made her eyebrow raise. "I have never seen you smile when talking to your brother." He responded, "Well, I do now." As the years went by, Alison was filled with a soft joy in knowing that her boys were now acting like brothers. They started seeing each other more. Weekend visits turned into week-long getaways. The brothers started planning how to go visit one another and entertain each other in the towns they lived. It was a scene that Alison could only dream of.

As Christmas approached, she became excited over having her boys back in the house together again with this newfound spirit. The boys now had wives and a few small children. Alison was now a grandmother. On Christmas Day, they all opened their gifts and celebrated with each other. Under the tree, however, was one more gift. It said, "To Mom, Sorry it took us so long . . ." Under the wrapping was a picture of her two boys as they were, and her two boys as they were now. It didn't say anything on the frame except for Psalm 133:1. Alison retrieved her Bible and began reading. Her eyes began to water as she had come to know that her prayer had been answered. What a joy it is when family can live together in harmony.

Lord, thank You for my family. Allow me to do everything that I can to maintain harmony with them. Allow me to be able to grow deeper relationships with them so that this harmony will be a lasting one.

95

Light Cannot Be Overcome

That light shines in the darkness,
yet the darkness did not overcome it.
John 1:5

In Kentucky, there is a cavern that gives tours in complete darkness. Mammoth Cave is the largest cave system in the world. It is one of the natural wonders in this country that gains nearly two million visitors each year. What is astonishing about this cave is the specific style of tours that are given. Once a tour is in the deepest part of the cave, they turn off the lights so that the visitors can feel what it is like to be in total darkness. Some have described it as being one of the most overwhelming feelings in the world. Because of this specific brand of darkness, they cannot even tell what is inches away from their faces. Your senses begin to over compensate for your body's loss of sight. One tourist spoke on how she could only tell her hand was inches away from her face because of the heat that it was giving off. It is one of the most awe-inspiring parts of the entire tour. Guides will even go to the trouble of recommending that glowing articles of clothing should not be brought because even the faintest light will hinder the experience of total darkness. Even the smallest flicker or spark will ruin the experience.

There is something to be said about that. That even in a place where darkness should rule, the smallest source of light cannot be overcome. Light is one of the most fascinating properties of this world. It is the only thing on this planet that darkness cannot overcome. Even if all of the shadows of all the world were to converge on a single flame, a candle would not be overtaken. We search for it when storms start to gain power. We move toward it when our back is to the darkness. Some of us, if we're honest, still sprint toward it after turning off the lights in another room. Why do we do this? It's because of the fact that we have come to know that light is something that will always be stronger than darkness. It holds the ability to give hope and security even in the darkest of times.

Light has the ability to make us feel safe. It has the ability to make us feel secure. We use it to find what is lost. We use it to see what cannot be seen with our own eyes. Light reveals. It eliminates shadow. It is the ultimate overcomer, and can never be overcome. We can take joy in knowing that God provides a light that not only shines in darkness, but overcomes darkness to the point where it doesn't exist.

Thank You for being the light of my life. Thank You for providing a light for me in the dark moments. Allow me to constantly be aware of the love that You give each day, and remind me to share the light You have given me with others.

96

You Cannot Ignore His Path for You

Many plans are in a man's heart,
but the LORD's decree will prevail.
PROVERBS 19:21

~

A mother always has a bit of an instinct over the future of her children. One mother in particular always knew that her son would be a pastor. She first had this feeling whenever she picked him up from the park. She saw him standing on the see-saw talking about what he had learned in Sunday school. She watched him grow up in the church and become a leader to others.

When it came time for college, the mother asked her son what he would do. He said that he wanted to major in athletic training. For him, it was good money, and he would be able to make a living out of his fitness hobbies. The mother, however, said, "Don't do that." The boy looked at her with surprise, but she explained, "I really think that you should go into the ministry. You've always been so caring for others, and you've always been a large part of the leadership of the church even at such a young age." The boy looked at his mother, and said, "There's no money in ministry. Plus, I can still serve the church and be an athletic trainer." The mother sighed, but agreed that he should do what he thinks is best.

The young man was very successful as an athletic trainer. He had made his own business and was only working four days out of the week. He was doing considerably well for himself, but no matter how much money he made or how flexible his schedule was, he could not shake the feeling that he was doing something wrong. It was not that he felt like he was sinning as an athletic trainer. It was just that he simply felt he was not doing what he was meant to do. He recalled his mother's words, but shook his head and continued on the path of his business venture.

After a few more years, he was married, had a child, and was looking to retire in ten or fifteen years. It seemed that his life was as it should be. All of this, however, would change every time he saw his mother. She could always tell that something was in his mind. Like most mothers, she always had an intuition for when her son was bothered by something. With a frustrated look on his face, he shook his head and said, "Mom, I think you might have been right. I have everything I could ever want. God has blessed me. I love my job. I have a beautiful family, but I never have a sense of joy when I walk in the gym as when I walk into the Lord's house."

He started ministering to the people of the church in an unofficial manner—leading Bible studies, being a leader in certain ministries, and so on. All the while, he was back in school educating himself on the Bible in a more formal setting. After a few years, he completed his education and was eventually given the opportunity to minister as a staff member of the church he had been attending. During his first sermon, he looked out to the congregation and said, "Folks, listen to your Mothers. They're the only ones who know you almost as much as God."

God, allow me to listen to You.
Direct my path, and allow me to follow.

97

Don't Go Alone

Two are better than one because they have a good reward
for their efforts. For if either falls, his companion can lift him
up; but pity the one who falls without another to lift him up.
ECCLESIASTES 4:9–10

A sport that is often overlooked by the more traditional sports is that of cross-country. It is a running sport where student compete individually and as a team. For instance, one team can have the fastest runner that would have the best individual time in a race, but another team could win if more of them place higher than other teams. So, even though it may be beneficial to have a runner that is incredibly fast, it is almost better to find a team of runner that perform well together.

Cross-country coaches will often be more focused on developing their team instead of an individual runner. It is better to sharpen all of them as a whole than just have them compete individually. The reason for this could not have been clearer when one of the runners twisted her ankle during practice. She was so focused on making a new record for herself that she had pulled away from the pack. This is normally not a problem, but for this specific instance, she learned a valuable lesson. Because she had decided to pull away from the pack, she found herself alone ten minutes after deciding to pick up her pace. When she fell, she found herself leaning against a tree that was off the path.

Why is this important? Ask any runner and they will tell you how easy it is to develop a tunnel vision while running; how there is an intense focus on what is in front of them to the point that they don't notice anything but the path. This is not to mention how frustrating it can be to get people's attention if they have headphones in their ears The only reason one of the other girls noticed something was wrong is because some of the gravel had been kicked off the trail and it caused her to look up from her trance. She was able to look a few feet off the trail and see her teammate. The rest of the team immediately ran to her side, a few ran back to get the coach, and the rest were able to sit with their teammate while they waited for the coach.

When the coach finally arrived, she scolded the injured player. "Do you realize how lucky you are? It could have been hours before we found you because you decided to break away from the team. There is a reason why we have teams. They are there to lift you up the moment you fall."

Trying to make it on our own is not something any of us should aspire to do, especially when God has blessed us with so many amazing people in our lives to catch us when we fall. God knows that we were never meant to be alone, so that in times when we fall, we always know that He has given us people to lift us to our feet.

Thank You for giving me helpers, Lord. Allow me to be willing
to stay with those who love me. Allow me to be willing
to be helped, and allow me to help others in their time of need.

98

Understanding Is a Product of Patience

A patient person shows great understanding,
but a quick-tempered one promotes foolishness.
Proverbs 14:29

⌒

It was Ashley's first time to help prepare the Christmas dinner. It was something she had dreamed of ever since she could remember. She was thirteen years old, and her mother told her that she could help any of the adults make whatever they were making. She was not ready to make something on her own. Ashley was known for being a little spontaneous. Out of all of the relatives, she wanted to help her grandmother make her famous monkey bread. It was her favorite thing to eat at Christmas, so why shouldn't she have a hand in making it?

Her grandmother gave her the ingredients and told her how to properly put them together. Ashley enjoyed the messy part, it was something that allowed her to feel personally involved in what she was doing. Something Ashley was not known for, however, was her patience. When it came time to bake, she was told to put the monkey bread into the oven at 350 degrees for around thirty-five minutes. Ashley, being impatient, put the oven at 450 degrees for 20 minutes. Any baker will probably tell you how incredibly unwise this is. To no one's surprise, it was a disaster. Ten minutes into the baking and the grandmother could smell something burning.

What happened next, however, is what truly captures the point of this whole story. Ashley came to her grandmother—frustrated as to what had happened, but the grandmother was not upset. She simply said, "Child, I was preparing another batch the moment you took it to the oven. Let's just try it again." The grandmother had developed a patience and understanding of people that allowed her to make predictions on the outcomes of some people's actions. Ashley, a little more at ease, asked her grandmother, "Why didn't you just put the oven where it should have been?" She responded with, "How would you ever learn how not to bake something if you didn't learn it firsthand?"

Ashley made the monkey bread again with her grandmother, the right way. She put it in at the right temperature for the right amount of time. When it came out, she realized that she had made the monkey bread with only a little bit of guidance from her grandmother. She was proud. It looked like her grandmother's, smelled like her grandmother's, and most importantly, tasted like her grandmother's monkey bread—so much so that her parents couldn't tell the difference.

God shows us the difference of outcomes when we act with a patient spirit instead of a quick-tempered one. Ashley was happy with her monkey bread. She would say that she was overjoyed, but she realized she could have had two helpings of the dessert if she had just acted with a patient spirit the first time.

Lord, allow me to have a patient spirit. Put in me a spirit of understanding. Remind me to not act with a quick temper.

99

Benefits of Kindness

A kind man benefits himself,
but a cruel man brings disaster on himself.
PROVERBS 11:17

Most small town churches have something called a meal train. It is where a few people in the church come together and prepare meals for those that are either dealing with loss or a family member is in the hospital. Carolyn, an older lady in the church, was the head of that train and was not known for messing around. She was always working to ensure that any person that found themselves in a difficult time did not have to worry about meals. She always made a dessert. That was her staple, but she often coordinated with other homes to ensure that whichever church member was in need, had their needs met.

The meal train came to be famous for a few years. It was the silver lining of sickness or loss. A member, at least, knew that there would be a meal and a dessert taken care of for a few days during a time of heartache. Carolyn saw it as her ministry. It was her passion to show kindness to those that were in a time of disaster.

When her husband was sick, she also got her meal needs met. She was overjoyed that the meal train even remembered their leader. It did not, however, replace the hurt. Her husband only became more ill. He took a slow decline until, finally, he went home to be with the Lord. Carolyn was devastated, but something that she noticed, even in this time of heartache, she never worried for a meal. During that time of sitting with her husband, she noticed something. She had never mowed the lawn. She had not taken out the trash. She had not really gone to the grocery store, and had never really had to fill up her tank. She had been so focused on her husband's health that she realized that not only did the world keep spinning, but the chores seemed to do themselves as well. It was then that she made a realization, all of the people that she had taken time to serve had all dedicated a hand to helping her. Her closest friend on the meal train took out her trash when she brought her meals. A young man that she had served owned a lawn care company that would swing by and mow her yard at no cost. The pastor's daughter would come by and water her plants while the pastor would go out and replenish her groceries. She had given many tears of sadness over losing her family, but they were soon replaced with tears of joy when she realized that she had a family that were already with her every step of the way. It was Carolyn's kindness that benefited her in ways she could never imagine.

> Remind me to be kind to others. Allow me to benefit
> those that have shown kindness to me. Allow me to show
> love and graciousness toward those that are in need of it.

100

Don't Just Hear It. Do It!

*But be doers of the word and
not hearers only, deceiving yourselves.*

JAMES 1:22

⌒

One of the most difficult things for us to hear is the necessity for us to act. Many of us can hear all of the right things and yet, never make a move. This is not just in regards to the Bible. We will have commercials tell us about losing weight, furthering our education, or saving money, and still, many of us will simply hear the message and not act on it. Do we ever realize just how much we miss out on because of our unwillingness to act, our unwillingness to do.

The greatest message we could ever hear is the message of the gospel. It is a message that tells us that we are loved, that there is a God who loves us so much that He gave His only Son for us so that we might escape death and have eternal life with Him. We have a God that sent down His Son to pay for the wages of our sin so that we might be blameless in the eyes of God, and that is only one of the messages in the Word of God.

We are told stories about how to love others, how to lead others, and how to chase after God. We are given words of wisdom on how to live our lives in a godly manner. We have poetry that shows us how to care and love for others. We have historical accounts that show the boldness of the men and women who chased after God. We have accounts of preachers and teachers that show us how to lead others to Christ and how to disciple them after we've helped them find Him. We have all of this screaming at us—demanding action from us, and even though we have all of this information at our fingertips with the direct purpose of being shared with others, we still lie to ourselves and say, "Not me, maybe someone else."

Do you realize the joy that God has for you? Do you acknowledge the power, wisdom, and love that comes from sharing the knowledge of the Word of God with others? Can you even ascertain all that God has for us out of His own love and mercy for us?

God has made us to be more than just hearers and readers. He has called us to be doers. So go out. Share the joy that has come from this book. Relay the happiness to others in hopes that they will understand what it is that makes you so joyful in the first place. God created you to be more, so go out and be more, and reveal the joy that comes with following after Him.

Thank You for making me more. Thank You for calling
me to be mighty. Allow me to share the wisdom and love
that You have given me, so others might know You.